THE RHYTHM
OF DISCIPLESHIP

Other books in the Foundations of Christian Faith series

THE RHYTHM
OF DISCIPLESHIP

Luther D. Ivory

Foundations of Christian Faith
Published by Geneva Press in Conjunction with
the Office of Theology and Worship, Presbyterian Church (U.S.A.)

Scripture quotations from the New Revised Standard Version of the Bible are copyright © 1989 by the Division of Christian Education of the National Council of the Churches of Christ in the U.S.A. and are used by permission.

Book design by Sharon Adams
Cover design by Night & Day Design

First edition
Published by Geneva Press
Louisville, Kentucky

This book is printed on acid-free paper that meets the American National Standards Institute Z39.48 standard. ∞

PRINTED IN THE UNITED STATES OF AMERICA

08 09 10 11 12 13 14 15 16 17 — 10 9 8 7 6 5 4 3 2 1

Library of Congress Cataloging-in-Publication Data
Ivory, Luther D.
    The rhythm of discipleship / Luther Ivory. — 1st ed.
       p. cm. — (Foundations of Christian faith)
    ISBN 978-0-664-50296-6 (alk. paper)
    1. Christian life.   2. Spiritual formation.   I. Title.
  BV4501.3.I96 2008
  248.4—dc22   2007031719

Contents

Series Foreword

*T*he books in the Foundations of Christian Faith series explore central elements of Christian belief. These books are intended for persons on the edge of faith as well as for those with strong Christian commitment. The writers are women and men of vital faith and keen intellect who know what it means to be an everyday Christian.

Each of the twelve books in the series focuses on a theme central to the Christian faith. The authors hope to encourage you as you grapple with the big, important issues that accompany our faith in God. Thus, Foundations of Christian Faith includes volumes on the Trinity, what it means to be human, worship and sacraments, Jesus Christ, the Bible, the Holy Spirit, the church, life as a Christian, political and social engagement, religious pluralism, creation and new creation, and dealing with suffering.

You may read one or two of the books that deal with issues you find particularly interesting, or you may wish to read them all in order to gain a deeper understanding of your faith. You may read the books by yourself or together with others. In any event, I trust that you will find a fuller awareness of the living God who is made known in Jesus Christ through the present power of the Holy Spirit. Christian faith is not about the mastery of ideas. It is about encountering the living God. It is my confident hope that this series of books will lead you more deeply into that encounter.

Charles Wiley
Office of Theology and Worship
Presbyterian Church (U.S.A.)

Acknowledgments

*W*hen a project has sustained a developmental process as lengthy as the present volume, the debts accumulated along by the author are bound to be too numerous to disclose in the minuscule space allotted. I do, however, believe that a moral imperative exists at least to attempt to publicly thank all those who have labored along the way, sharing their talents toward the end of bringing life to this text. While a list that offers a full accounting is simply too great a burden to produce, I would nevertheless like to offer gratitude to a few of the many remarkable human beings without whose efforts this book would never have experienced the pangs of birth. Charles Wiley, Theology Division, PC(USA), project conceptualizer and manager, deserves special thanks. His faith in me and his valuable commentary and motivation throughout the process have been outstanding. Frank Hainer's numerous editorial suggestions regarding content revision and stylistic approach have made the volume more accessible and intelligible. Other authors in this series, along with the Job-like patience of the WJK staff, have assisted me in getting back on track when I had lost my way. Several institutions have played an invaluable role in shaping my perspectives and deserve thanks: Douglass High, University of Tennessee, U.S. Army and Navy, Union Seminary, Emory University, Rhodes College, as well as my home churches: First Baptist Mt. Olive, Union Grove, New Harvest, St. Andrews, Peace Lutheran, and Parkway United. To the cadre of family nurturers, brothers and sisters, who encouraged me to persevere, especially Carole J. Tweetie, Tonka, and FuFee. Finally, to the Bungalo Braves, who taught me the value of belonging; my father, "Big Bill," who never let me get ahead of myself; and to my incomparable mother, the late Dorothy Mae Ivory, without whom this book could not even have been conceptualized, much less written. It was "Mama Dorothy" who provided the framework for my theological understanding of vocational call in a unique way, and for that and many other life lessons, I will be forever in her debt.

Memphis, Tennessee
April 2007

The Rhythm of Christian Discipleship

Call and Response

*The same Spirit . . . feeds us with the bread of life and the
cup of salvation, and calls women and men to all ministries of the church.*
A Brief Statement of Faith,
Book of Confessions, PC(USA)

The Invitation to Participatory Presence

When I think about organizing the division of labor in a large
family, no one did it like my mama. I remember growing up in a
family of eight children in north Memphis. "Mama Dorothy," as
my mother was affectionately known, identified, assessed, and
tapped the various skills resident in each of the Ivory children in
order to assist her in completing the heavy demands of the daily
agenda. Always problematic was being current on the status and
general location of each of the eight children at any given time.
Exacerbating this problem was our propensity for scattering in
all directions every chance we got. Consequently, whenever our
mother needed us, we were usually outside the sphere of immediate accessibility. What, then, was she to do? What mode of
communication would best allow her, regardless of our location,
to seize our attention and alert us to the fact that our presence was
required? This was a challenge of no mean proportions.

Undaunted, my mother worked out a rather unique communications system that allowed her both to effectively track our
whereabouts at any given time throughout the day and to summon

us, on demand, when we were needed. The heart of Mama Dorothy's system was to associate distinct vocal sounds with specific familial tasks, using a distinct phonetic identifier for each of her eight children. As a third-generation hog farmer, my mother was thoroughly familiar with the various grunts, snorts, and squeals that were prominent features in the long, Southern tradition of hog calling.

You can guess where this is going. With an amazing inventiveness, she managed to appropriate and refashion this assortment of porcine acoustics into a viable communications system that she then utilized effectively to summon us with quick dispatch. Whenever Mama Dorothy would cut loose with a sound that began with a long, shrill "eeeeeee!" the Ivory siblings recognized that she was signaling the boys to attention. Likewise, sounds begun with a short "oouuww!" signaled the girls. Having specified the gender, she would then employ a distinctive phonic identifier for the particular boy or girl she needed. Finally, my mother would utilize distinct nasal and guttural vocalizations to indicate the specific task for which the individual was subpoenaed. In this way my mother was able to alert any one of her children to carry out a specific task at any time.

Admittedly, this system was rather complicated and posed no small challenge for children of our ages, ranging from five to sixteen years. Mama Dorothy, though, was not in the least bit phased by the complexities involved in learning the system. She assembled us in a family circle around the dinner table and taught the system several times a day for about a month. She then coordinated seemingly endless rehearsals and daily pop quizzes until we had each demonstrated to her satisfaction that we were able to identify the various sounds and their meanings. We learned to differentiate between a call to perform routine household chores like emptying the trash or slopping the hogs, and a call to run some errand like going to the corner grocery or taking a plate of food to the home of one of the older, bedridden, neighborhood "wisdom carriers," as they were known. Of course, the system was not perfect. Sometimes we misheard or misinterpreted the various sounds. We thought we heard a call for an Ivory girl, but it was for an Ivory boy, or the wrong boy or girl would show up having mistaken someone else's phonic I.D. for their own. I remember once hearing a call, then running off to the neighborhood kerosene pumping station to bring home a can of kerosene oil for the house lamps, only to discover that I was actually supposed to pick up a bag of groceries at Johnson's Sundry.

Without question, the success of this system was significantly enhanced by the capacity of the Ivory children to hear the call, focus and listen carefully, accurately interpret the message, and respond with minimal delay. Each time we managed to succeed, good things invariably happened, and the entire family benefited.

To be sure, this communication system represented an extraordinary feat of human ingenuity requiring huge amounts of energy, creativity, and practice. Even now, I marvel not only at my mother's ability to conceptualize and implement it, but also at the children's willingness to master the system. When I reflect upon these boyhood experiences, I see in them important clues for understanding the nature of Christian discipleship as an alternating rhythm of divine call and human response. I now understand that, like Mama Dorothy, God also calls each of us in the family of faith in different ways, at different times, to participate in differing ministries. This call, in effect, provides countless opportunities for us to offer our various talents in service to God's agenda for the church and the world. I also see how crucial active listening is in the invitational rhythm of call and response for the Christian disciple as it was for the Ivory children in their family life. The disciple has to be able to hear God's call and accurately discern that call's demands on his or her life if he or she is to make a faithful response to the invitation. Sometimes we Ivory children would confuse our mother's various calls and show up in the wrong place. We each had to learn to distinguish our own, unique call from the myriad of sounds heard throughout each day. Further, since my mother called a particular child for a particular task, we also had to learn to accurately identify the specific sound associated with each task.

Some calls issued by Mama Dorothy were recognized as general ones, applicable to every child in the Ivory family. One such was the call to the dinner table. Every evening, my mother would open the screen door at the rear of our home, lean out, and let loose a series of oral alerts. These stylized vocalizations involved the use of several long guttural whelps followed immediately by a crescendo of three short, staccato yells: "n-a-a—y-I, n-a-a—y-I yuch yuch yuch!" Every

Ivory child knew the exact meaning of that unique combination of sounds: supper was ready. Within minutes, we would arrive panting and stand in prearranged formation at the gate. After washing, we entered and sat at our designated place at the table. Each child then recited his or her weekly assigned Bible verse from memory. Finally, the person who had been privileged to serve as the week's grace sayer prayed over the food, then we ate.

As a boy, I was unaware of the rather profound theological and ethical implications of this experience. In retrospect, I now see that the combined experiences of Mama Dorothy's daily calling of the household to dinner and the subsequent gathering of our family at the kitchen table embodied our participation in a special, sacramental moment. A sacrament may be defined as an outward, visible sign of an inner, invisible grace. In other words, a sacrament is an outward experience that confirms the reality of an unmerited favor toward us. In such an event, we may discern that God is with us, moving among us, acting with and for us, continuously calling us to participate in a more intimate relationship with God and one another. In this way we may experience, as did the prophet Isaiah in the temple, the powerful presence of God, inviting us to a deeper participation in a reality that endures beyond human existence.

> In the year that King Uzziah died, I saw the LORD sitting on a throne, high and lofty; and the hem of his robe filled the temple. Seraphs were in attendance above him; each had six wings: with two they covered their faces, and with two they covered their feet, and with two they flew. And one called to another and said:
>
> "Holy, holy, holy is the LORD of hosts;
> the whole earth is full of his glory."
> Isaiah 6:1–3

We come to know ourselves more fully as God knows us. We may glimpse more clearly the purpose for which God has made us. Our awareness of God's continual inbreaking into human affairs may be significantly heightened.

Revelatory moments may occur in but are not limited to the corporate celebration of Eucharist or baptism. Any moment may become revelatory in the sense that it mediates an unseen, active spiritual presence through visible human activity. Hence sacramental moments may occur in activities that may have little to do with ecclesial life: engaging in a moment of honest conversation with a stranger; asking for and receiving forgiveness from a coworker for a wrong you have committed; visiting with a person who is terminal with HIV-AIDS; making a phone call to an individual who is struggling and suffering privately through a long, intense grief process; experiencing the power of a live concert; working as a member of some organization that is pursuing economic or social justice; sharing a meal.

The elements involved in sacramental moments include: God's active presence among us inviting our participation, our openness to that presence, our capacity to discern that presence, and our willingness to accept the invitation offered through the experience. This concrete participation in and with divine presence helps define our piety. Participation in a sacramental moment enlivens our relationship with God.

As I look back on it, the very act of my mother's calling, as well as the shared experience of our family's daily gatherings to break bread at the dinner table, represented daily, sacramental moments. That is, these activities were visible signs of an invisible love and grace at work in both our individual and family life. Though well beyond either our awareness or comprehension, those daily experiences provided glimpses into what it means to live one's life as a response to a reality greater than oneself, a reality that makes morally compelling demands upon one's time and talents, symbolizing what it means to live one's life as a moral agent and community member, accountable to others for what one does or does not do. Therefore, what appeared on the surface as casual, bland, and mundane was in fact public enactment of our family's invisible journey of encounter, struggle, transformation, reinterpretation, and rededication. Without our having to earn it, we were called each day and invited to sit at a table prepared by someone we knew loved us unconditionally. This was not an invitation from a noncommittal stranger offered out of duty; this call came from our mother, a person with whom we enjoyed an intimate, loving relationship. It was our special relationship with her that prompted our active, wholehearted response.

It was precisely those elements of mercy, grace, and love that accompanied both my mother's call to the table and the sharing of the meal itself that made those experiences uniquely special. Indeed, these added ingredients elevated our daily gathering beyond the commonplace realm of ordinary occurrence and into the sublime level of a sacramental moment. Of course, I am convinced that unconditional love and grace were involved in each of the meals we shared daily. However, neither breakfast nor lunch offered the qualitatively unique experience for our family that dinnertime provided. First, there was no unique phonic call for either breakfast or lunch. Second, we rarely gathered en masse as a family around the kitchen table to eat breakfast or lunch. We were left to our own discretion in these meals. My mother merely prepared the food and left it on the stove in covered dishes. It was the intentionally structured communal approach of the dinner meal that significantly enhanced the possibilities for us to experience a shared sacramental moment.

Although I did not understand it at the time, the sacramental nature of my mother's invitation to the dinner meal and our response to that call offered some important insights into the way Christian discipleship works. The basic motivation of the dinner meal was not merely the need to fill empty stomachs but the wonderful love of my mother that provided the basis of her stewardship in the ministry of feeding. Unmerited favor and unconditional love motivated her rather than any social pressure, legal coercion, or the performance of obligatory, domestic duties. I cannot recall a single time when any of us experienced her invitational call to the dinner table as a coercive, dictatorial command. Attraction, not coercion, elicited our response.

In the same way, God's way of relating to the disciple is through redeeming grace and unconditional love. God's call to the disciple is not the bark of a drill sergeant who terrorizes recruits through fear, intimidation, threat, and punishment; rather, like Mama Dorothy, God calls, we respond. God does not pressure, coerce, or force our response; discipleship is by invitation only. God's call has nothing in common with mean-spirited proselytizing.

Sacramental moments, when the grace of God is vouchsafed to us, by their very nature always bring with them a call, an invitation to decide for alternative visions of life and modes of thinking. In this sense, a sacramental moment is never without some inner tension, deliberation, and the demands of responsible decision making. Viewed in this sacramental context, I now understand that our response to my mother's call was never merely a personal decision negotiated between each individual child and my mother. Nor was our response solely a matter of private resolution between each of us and the urgent reality of our growling stomachs. Rather, our response was a public statement of our acceptance of our mother's love and grace. It was also a corporate confession of our need of her grace and nurture. It was a communal expression of our acknowledgment of her right as a responsible parent to be intimately present and engaged with us. It also served as a collective affirmation of our mother's right to make urgent, responsible, and inescapable moral demands on each of us as well. Without question, Mama Dorothy had demonstrated her unfailing commitment to our welfare daily over the years of our lives. We not only believed in her capabilities as a mother, but we also trusted her motives, accepted her judgments, and abided by her decisions. We were absolutely convinced of her love and positive valuation of each of us, and we knew that her primary objective was the promotion of our dignity, health, and happiness. This knowledge alone prompted our willingness to follow wherever she led us, and to carry out, to the best of our abilities, whatever task she assigned.

It is certainly true that our daily self-presentations at the backyard gate were driven by both the pangs of hunger and sheer gratitude for the privilege of dinner. Yet what appeared then to be a solely private matter in the politics of personal decision making was actually a choice for membership and participation in the communal dynamics of family living. As we each accepted the invitation to dinner, we acknowledged, at the same time, our responsibility to concern ourselves with the issues deemed important to the family. We made a public commitment to worry about and to address those needs most pressing upon each family member. What seemed, at that time, a matter of private choice and individual concern was in reality a communal moment that drew us into the life of a larger community.

At first glance, the invitation posed no heavy challenge or unrealistic expectations for any of us. We needed to bring only our appetites and a willingness to actively participate in the conversation and the meal. In retrospect, however, one can see that once gathered at the table, we found that the invitation brought with it heavier responsibilities; it included broader and more profound implications for our life together as a family. Further, I now realize that the invitation to dinner was ultimately a request for our participation in a communal meal rather than an offer simply to stuff ourselves. It was at the table, in full engagement with the family, that the meal became a symbol of both our inclusion in and commitment to the family. Indeed, our choice to attend that dinner was a public decision for membership and belonging.

This insight reveals something significant about the nature of Christian discipleship: it is a communal experience. Commitment to the lordship of Jesus Christ and development as a disciple are not possible in isolation. No one can lay claim to discipleship as a lone journeyer. The intensely social nature of the Christian faith requires the embrace of a gregarious relational style in order to maximize spiritual formation and development. Becoming a Christian disciple is something none of us can achieve alone, isolated from the support and guidance of others. As with each Ivory child, each Christian seeker depends upon a community, a family of faith that sustains, nurtures, and facilitates assimilation into the tradition. We all need companions on the journey of discipleship. Discipleship ministry depends upon the collective efforts of all our individual gifts. This understanding critiques and corrects current cultural notions about overly individualistic, privatized, and interiorized expressions of faith and spirituality. The communal nature of the Ivory dinner taught me that discipleship does not reduce to a merely private relationship with the Christ. "Me and my Jesus" walking together in the garden of life, apart from the rest of the human community, does not square with the New Testament witness. Discipleship is a shared, social experience. As with the Ivory children at the dinner meal, our growth as individual members of the household of faith is existentially impossible apart from genuine interaction with others.

Paul's correspondence to the Christian communities at Corinth and Ephesus speaks precisely to this issue. In chapter 12 of 1 Corinthians, using the metaphor of the human body, the apostle lifts up the organic nature of the faith family, and points out that the survival, growth, and effectiveness of the church's mission are based upon the dynamic interaction of all its members. When the contributions of all its members are mutually honored and equally valued, the entire community becomes the beneficiary. By pooling diverse gifts and talents and working together, the community is able to accomplish more than any one of its parts. Notice, though, that when Paul turns to the Ephesian community (Ephesians 4), he expands the underlying theme of unity found in the Corinthians text. He makes explicit the connection between group maintenance and task. The purpose of unity in the family is not only to effect the spiritual growth of its individual members and the nurturing of relationships in the ecclesial body politic, but also to enhance the operational readiness of the church to actively engage the work of the ministry to which it is called. Later, in Ephesians 6, Paul makes clear that the work of ministry indeed involves an intense struggle against malevolent and destructive forces at work in the world. Paul views the church's ministry of shared social responsibility as an essential part of its *nature*. The church family looks both inward and outward.

Paul's counsel to the Corinthians and Ephesians helps illuminate the deeper meaning of my family's dinner activities. We were acutely aware that an invitation to convene at the table was certainly a great privilege. In time, we learned that along with great privilege comes great responsibility. I am sure that we never fully comprehended all the subtler and more profound ethical implications of the experience. However, it slowly dawned upon us that responding positively to Mama Dorothy's invitational call to dinner involved much more than a choice for consumption. Along with fine food, our choice had resulted in our becoming participants in causes that were larger than our individual selves.

As we gathered at the table, additional demands were made upon each of us. We learned to anticipate that whenever we arrived at the table new calls might be issued. Sometimes the new calls would result in a reassignment of tasks, as when my sister Brenda began taking flute lessons after school. Normally, she was assigned the task of picking up six-year-old Kay Kay (her name was Karen, but we called her Kay Kay) from the Garners, where she played each day with a friend. Brenda's flute lessons made this arrangement impossible. Because of his acknowledged dependability, my brother William was reassigned this task, and I, in turn, took over his former assignment of stopping by each day to check up on and run errands for Mr. Troy Finley (a hemiplegic senior citizen who lived alone in our neighborhood). At other times, newly issued calls resulted in completely novel assignments, as when another senior citizen, Miss Mattie Logan, suffered a mild stroke. Although she regained partial use of her limbs, she still required daily assistance in small tasks such as cleaning up beverage spills, emptying trash containers, sweeping and mopping floors, washing dishes, ironing, or cleaning the toilet. Since my sister Gerceta was the oldest of the children, she drew this additional assignment as part of her regular daily tasks. My brother Fred took over the biweekly delivery of groceries to the home of Mr. Columbus Hayes (yet another infirm senior citizen living in our community) from Johnson's Sundry. As we eventually figured out, at the Ivory household, the to-do list was never final. There were always more calls to action, more work to be done.

The dinner table experience, in essence, amounted to an authentic encounter with the core content of an overarching and compelling family agenda with its values, ideals, objectives, and commitments. That daily encounter decisively shaped our sense of both individual and collective identities as well as our individual perceptions of the world around us, our notions of the true and the good, and our perspectives on how to cope with the realities we faced. Our participation in the daily ritual of call and response invited us to struggle and explore, choose and surrender, clarify and rededicate personal time and talents to causes much larger than our individual selves. Identity formation, character building, goal setting, and lifestyle commitments all derived from our involvement in the ritual and rhythm of call and response.

Gradually we came to understand that in terms of priority, the composite needs and objectives of the Ivory family ranked higher in importance than those of any one of its members. We were each expected to surrender our personal agendas and to rearrange our individual priorities in accordance with those of the family. The experience of invitation to and sharing at the dinner table decisively promoted an ethic of responsibility that shaped how we structured our family life. This ethic functioned as a moral compass, orienting us toward the development of a more communal consciousness and lifestyle that countered the more insidious individualist tendencies operating in our midst. Further, while this ethic of responsibility certainly contributed to our family's particular collective self-understanding, it extended beyond the identity issue. The ethic also significantly influenced relational patterns and interaction within the Ivory family, as well as our mode of active engagement in and with members of the neighborhood in which we lived.

Without question, a lot more was going on at the Ivory family dinner table than a mere gathering at the trough. Each person's choice to be present somehow signaled an agreement to bond as a family, to value one another's gifts, to respect and uphold one another's dignity, to participate in one another's lives, to be concerned about one another's welfare. Each day, in a manner akin to confirmation services in the church, our presence at the table initiated a ritual of public reaffirmation. This time together marked our period of rededication during which we each confirmed previously stated covenants of solidarity. In effect, we each reestablished communal links, and in this way served to strengthen the cohesion of the family unit. What were we really saying to one another? Ultimately, we were saying that prior commitments to assume mutual responsibility were binding and worth honoring. We were saying that every individual had to be interpreted within the boundaries of a communal structure. We were saying that our legitimate personal needs, priorities, and values could not stand independently from our communal obligations. We did not merely eat, get up, and leave without any acknowledgment of the ties that bound us together in solidarity as members of the household. Rather, we publicly offered support for those we had accepted as our brothers and sisters. We recognized and affirmed the value of these kinship ties at each gathering. In reality, our mother's dinner invitation was a subtle but powerful call to wrestle with the nature of life together as a member of the Ivory household. An affirmative response of "Yes, I accept!" was tantamount to a choice to covenant together to explore issues of identity (who am I?) and ethics (what am I to do?) in light of a publicly acknowledged membership in this family.

The Ivory family experience of call and response, especially with regard to the dinner table, offers a metaphor for discipleship. The experience of living in an intimate, covenantal relationship under the lordship of Jesus Christ begins, as did my family's daily experiences at the dinner table, with an invitation. Jesus said to Matthew, "Follow me," and Matthew got up and followed him (Matt. 9:9). The two movements in the rhythm of discipleship are thus invitational call and response. The first movement is solely divine initiative: the call of

God upon the human community, a call to embark upon a journey of discovery into a new and right relationship with God. The second movement involves the human response to the divine call. With this comes new insights about God, self, and world that offer new possibilities for human existence. In Christian discipleship human activity is always a dependent variable, God's divine activity being the independent variable, prerequisite for any subsequent human action.

The rhythm of discipleship contains the powerful elements of challenge, critique, transformation, and redemption, which carry profound implications for both the individual believer and the church. A discipleship commitment places serious, unavoidable demands on the lives of disciples. The nature of discipleship involves a commitment to seeking, learning, and following the way of truth and love. The invitation to discipleship, like my mother's call to dinner, is always at the same time a challenge to participate in something more. Those who accept the invitation to join the community of faithful disciples gradually discover new possibilities for thinking, living, and becoming.

The individual call and response of the Christian disciple is a community event. God's call is mediated through a body of already-existing disciples called the church. This community of believers lives in the world. Christ commissioned the first believers to "Go therefore and make disciples of all nations" (Matt. 28:19). The church has effected this relationship with the world in a variety of ways. Presbyterian Christians have tended to interpret it in a dynamic way. The Presbyterian Constitution describes the primary tasks of the church vis-à-vis the world in this way: "The great ends of the church are the proclamation of the gospel for the salvation of humankind; the shelter, nurture, and spiritual fellowship of the children of God; the maintenance of divine worship; the preservation of the truth; the promotion of social righteousness; and the exhibition of the Kingdom of Heaven to the world."[1]

Pursuing these ends has always lent a profoundly social character to the ministry of the Presbyterian Church. One sees immediately how the "preservation of the truth, the promotion of social righteousness, and the exhibition of the Kingdom of Heaven to the world" demand awareness of the current cultural and political situation, discernment of God's will for the world, and courage to engage in the struggle "not against enemies of blood and flesh, but against the rulers, against the authorities, against the cosmic powers of this present darkness, against the spiritual forces of evil in the heavenly places" (Eph. 6:12).

Pursuing these great ends of the church commits disciples to engaging in the transformation of society as well as in true worship. Personal spiritual growth issues in regular prayer, weekly or monthly Eucharist, evangelism, and works of love and charity in the world in Christ's name that include courageous witness for justice and peace. The faithfulness of a local church's commitment to pursue the great ends of the church may be judged by the degree to which it enables its members to pursue these activities.

Discipleship is both individual and corporate. There is a warp and woof between private and public, individual and corporate, in Christian discipleship. There is a vertical movement of the divine/human relationship and the horizontal movement between human and human. Jesus expressed the critical importance of both dimensions in his teaching, for example, his summary of the law as love of both God and neighbor (Matt. 22:34–40). In the parable of the man who fell among thieves (Luke 10:25–37), Jesus defines the neighbor as the one who needs your help. This could apply to anyone, but Jesus puts special emphasis on the poor, the captive, and the oppressed (Luke 4:18). Any attempt to separate the individual and social dimensions of cross bearing fractures the Christian life. An affirmative response to the divine invitation initiates a piety characterized by both prayer without ceasing and the struggle for peace, love, and justice in the public square. Saying yes to God is always just the beginning, not the end, of discipleship. It is but a prelude to seeing the world through God's eyes.

Relating to God through worship, praise, prayer, singing, preaching, and sacraments generates an inseparable concern with living out that relationship through a social ethic informed by the gospel. A proper relationship with God expresses itself in establishing relationships with others characterized by love, justice, and peace. The act of responding to God's call to righteousness compels the disciple to live out God's will for human community, doing justice and seeking righteousness in the world. A proactive engagement with the power structures, ideological forces, and institutional arrangements of the world is an unavoidable component of Christian discipleship. It is, simply put, part of what God calls us to do as disciples. I believe that the call-and-response rhythm of discipleship means that spiritual discipline has as much to do with the distribution and use of money, land, public policy, power, and other social, political, and economic goods as it does with the practice of prayer, meditation, and Bible study. As the Scriptures indicate, the divine call to discipleship includes a compelling mandate for both individuals and groups to proactively engage the world powers in order to establish and advance God's agenda of righteousness. This agenda, as we shall see, includes the redemption of the institutional structures of society as well as the interior dispositions and inclinations of the hearts and souls of individuals who have committed to the lordship of Christ. In the final analysis, the call of God to discipleship always includes "speaking truth to power" and "the promotion of social righteousness, and the exhibition of the Kingdom of Heaven to the world." Spiritual commitments in response to the call of God divorced from responsible, love-based, justice-oriented, and reconciliation-promoting social action remain incomplete.

Jazz Rhythms and Christian Discipleship

One bitterly cold January night in 1997, I drove with a group of enthusiastic music lovers to the Precious Cargo Club in Memphis for another type of family assembly, a gathering of jazz musicians and connoisseurs. The Memphis Hepcats, a popular local jazz quintet, were in rare form that night, performing works of some of the masters of jazz history: John Coltrane, Miles Davis, Ella Fitzgerald, Duke Ellington, Count Basie, Sarah Vaughn, Lester Young, Dizzy Gillespie, and Wynton Marsalis. As I watched and listened, I began to see an implicit connection between the structure and method of jazz and the rhythmic nature of Christian discipleship.

Launching into one of my all-time favorite tunes, John Coltrane's arrangement of Rodgers and Hammerstein's "My Favorite Things," the band began by playing through the standard, familiar melody. They played the Coltrane arrangement from the sheet music in front of them that provided the basic structure of this rhythmically complex work, outlining the various parts for each instrument. As the musicians played, however, the highly improvisational nature of jazz began to emerge. With increasing sophistication, the group deviated from the original into an unbelievably creative interpretive rendition. With a myriad of novel chord changes and syncopated beats, something different emerged that was yet faithful to the original score. The band members carved out space so that each individual musician could break away from an already complicated composition and pour his own unique solo effort into the mix. The saxophonist played a wildly innovative riff or "feel" for a full six minutes as the quintet adapted chords, notes, and beats to stay "in the pocket" with his spontaneous, virtuoso performance.

A jazz musician must not only master his or her own individual instrument but also possess keen, active listening skills. Each band member depends upon all the others to offer their own unique instrumental parts in collaboration with the company to make the composition come alive. I noticed that when the music became more improvisational and the individual solo efforts were introduced, the musicians not only had to listen but also to trust one another's talents and judgments. Talking to the trumpet player after the set, I learned that the band really never knew in advance what the individual musicians were going to play or how they were going to play it. As he described it, a musician feeds off the energy generated by the music and the crowd response. Further, the artist is encouraged to be creative and innovative, and is expected to experiment with novel ideas while performing. Hence the solo offerings, I discovered, were always serendipitous to both soloist and band members. The bassist pointed out that it is important to understand that the actions of one instrumentalist have a profound impact on what the other band members will do. When a musician spontaneously reformulates and begins to play different notes, chords, or solo riffs, this change elicits yet another call to the other players to readjust and refashion their own parts. The need to listen, trust, and remain flexible is intrinsic to playing jazz. Musicians come to expect that the same composition will almost never be played exactly the same way. When I returned to the club two nights later, the band offered an entirely different rendition of "My Favorite Things." This time it was the trumpet player who took center stage, combining licks borrowed from Wynton Marsalis, Louis Armstrong, Charlie Parker, and Miles Davis for eight full minutes in a fascinating display of power and grace. As with the first performance two nights earlier, the band never lost sight of the basic structure of the original composition, which was heard as a constant "hook" or refrain for the duration of the twenty-four-minute performance of the tune.

A jazz composition consists of an assortment of notes, syncopated beats, and complex chord arrangements that are structured in such a way as to provide an interpretive framework that encourages diverse melodic expressions. The solo riffs of a particular jazz musician take place within a complex musical grid that provides contours and coordinates that guide individual expression. The overall melodic and rhythmic structure of a jazz composition functions as the musical call that initiates a musical response from each musician, who plays creatively with a wide degree of latitude. The individual musician plays within a community of musical discourse that structures individual expression. Thus, while jazz encourages creativity and improvisation, there are still definite parameters of musical expression. In this way the very structure of a jazz composition establishes a rhythm of call and response. The call evokes both individual and group response. The call also provides guidelines for acceptable behavior while, at the same time, allowing for a variety of responsive musical expression. Along with the basic compositional structure, the varied responses of individual musicians also act to call or prompt the remaining players to innovatively reconceptualize and refashion their individual solo responses.

In a similar manner, Christian discipleship operates within a particular community with its own unique call-and-response rhythm. As in jazz, the rhythm of call and response, question and answer, invitation and acceptance creates and maintains its own structured, interpretive framework. Just as the original score operates as the framework in jazz, so God's call, in concert with the biblical narrative, establishes the framework for the disciples' response. The call asks disciples of every stripe for an acceptance of and commitment to a core of fundamental values, ideas, ideals, and objectives. Disciples eat from the same table and play their instruments from the same original score. At the same time, the call encourages novelty and diversity in the expressions of both individuals and community. There is room at the table and within the band for interpretive differences. Freedom of individual perspectives exists. Disciples are not compelled to develop a single mentality or embrace a narrowly circumscribed set of beliefs and goals.

Yet the disciple cannot develop apart from the sustaining community. Rather, discipleship flourishes within a particular Christian community and expresses itself in both that nurturing fellowship and in acts of love and charity in the world beyond the gathered community. Disciples need the support and companionship of others in living out the demands of faith. No disciple becomes what he or she is all by him- or herself. It does take a village to raise a disciple. There has to be an investment and an involvement in the lives of others. There has to be listening to other voices, a trusting in one another's gifts, a willingness to learn from one another's contributions, a valuing of one another's uniqueness and individuality, and a playing off one another's strengths.

The rhythm of discipleship begins with God's invitation but does not end there. When a person accepts the invitation, more is at stake than merely becoming an insider. The objective of discipleship is not merely privilege of membership with all its benefits: nurture, fellowship, growth, companionship. Like the musicians in the jazz quintet, being in the community places unavoidable demands on the time and talents of the disciple to use his or her gifts with others toward the realization of a vision that is larger than any of the individual members. A faithful response may require a revolutionary shift in the way the disciple sees and interprets reality. In other words, authentic membership in a family, band, or church involves a *metanoia* experience. *Metanoia* means a transformation of the heart, literally a change of mind. *Metanoia* involves an alteration of perspective characterized by a conversion in the way one thinks and acts. While the sibling, musician, or disciple does effect changes in the dynamics of the group, the history, tradition, and shared ethos of the group exerts powerful influences on the member to reshape individual consciousness.

If the new disciple submits to the spiritual discipline of the community of faith, he or she may expect new insight into spiritual matters, new knowledge about the human condition, and discernment of what had been either previously hidden or dimly perceived. On the question of natural theology and whether humans can discern the true God with unaided reason purely from nature, John Calvin argued that we cannot. The marks of God are clearly there but only in an ephemeral way: "Since the notion of God as the mind of the universe (in the philosopher's eyes, a most acceptable description) is ephemeral, it is important for us to know him more intimately."[2] We need, Calvin says, the "spectacles" of Scripture to discern God rightly: "For just as eyes, when dimmed with age or weakness or by some other defect, unless aided by spectacles discern nothing distinctly; so, such is our feebleness, unless Scripture guides us in seeking God, we are immediately confused."[3] The new relationship with God, generated by a response to God's call and nurtured by the faith community, reshapes the individual's perspective on reality, as if the disciple were given a new set of "spectacles" that allow for a fuller disclosure of God's active presence in the world. It is the inner working of the Holy Spirit in the heart, mind, and soul of the individual believer that provides new sight. Yet this newly acquired gift cannot be fully sustained apart from continuous fellowship with the gathered community of faith. In time, the connection between inner and outer, private and public, personal and communal, priestly and prophetic will become more apparent to the disciple.

2

A Plea for Engaged Piety

*T*he continuing dilemma for Christian discipleship is how to balance inner change and outward action for social transformation. The church has dealt with this issue in a variety of ways through history. It comes down to how the church understands its role in society.

The Invitational Dilemma

Dieter Hessel's discussion of social ministry is helpful in illuminating the nature of the invitational dilemma.[1] He points out that in its attempts at communal self-definition, the church has historically experienced conflict with regard to its true nature and purpose. Two perspectives dominate how it should respond to various social contexts: private and public Christianity. Private Christianity is driven fundamentally by an understanding of spirituality that emphasizes revivalism and individualism. It welcomes into the church family individuals who have met Jesus and focuses heavily on nurturing within them a personal relationship with the God of love. Private-oriented spirituality, while not totally ignoring its social responsibility, tends to approach social needs from the standpoint of addressing personal sins and moral defects and condemning societal vices. Hessel argues that this form of spirituality leads to crusading and single-issue politics while sponsoring programs of service oriented to individual needs. It offers very little on social involvement with public issues of economic injustice and structural discrimination related to race, gender, or class. Persons who embrace this historical perspective may be identified as "rescuers."

Contrasted with this perspective is "public Christianity." Its adherents may be called "transformers." This perspective interprets biblical faith as a mandate to work actively for the redemption and transformation of the world. This tradition honors the necessity for personal nurturing and individual spiritual growth, but also demands that we critique and challenge the dominant culture, urging believers to work for social change where necessary to affect unjust human institutions. It sees the whole of reality as under the judgment and grace of God, and strives to restructure all human relationships in accordance with the social vision of the kingdom of God. Hessel is quick to point out that these two orientations cannot necessarily be distinguished on the basis of action or inaction. Both act. Rather, it is the type of active response in the society that differentiates them.

It is not a question of whether one or the other of these perspectives represents the correct response of the believer to society. Authentic biblical spirituality includes both perspectives. For a particular church to leave one or the other out is to truncate its ministry. The goal of transforming the social order must not overlook or forget the task of individual spiritual growth; the quest for interior spiritual discernment must not stop at individual enlightenment but continue into the realm of social change.

This in no way discounts the person who makes a moral decision to disengage and withdraw from social contact and seek a life of monastic asceticism. Such personal responses have been present throughout the church's history and represent valid options in the church's ministry tradition. Obviously, a different set of guidelines applies in such situations. What we have addressed above concerns the responses of people who accept the call of God to become part of the church family and continue to live in the workaday world. These people face the challenge of living out their faith commitment in a modern society full of ambiguity, greed, temptation, and violence. For such persons, accepting the invitation to dine at the table or play in the band may involve much more than pursuing personal, spiritual growth only, however necessary such growth is. As the reality of the cross and Jesus' words remind us, the inner, contemplative life of spiritual formation remains incomplete and disingenuous unless it is complemented by intentionality in working to establish relationships of love, justice, and peace in the human community. Faith without justice-oriented social action remains incomplete and morally wounded. By the same token, for the disciple, social action, even in the pursuit of justice, while morally proper, must also be informed by the spiritual resources of the faith. Without this continuous guidance by the Holy Spirit, social action itself becomes ultimately hollow and devoid of sustaining and transforming power.

An affirmative response to the invitational call of discipleship ought to mark the beginning of a lifelong journey with others encountering both inner and outer existential realities, and aiming at both personal redemption and social transformation, a journey that takes the individual beyond self into an encounter with a larger family, and beyond that family to an encounter with the world. A problem occurs when one side or the other of this encounter is short-circuited.

The rhythm of discipleship, then, includes a call to take seriously the moral necessity of proactive engagement in the affairs of human history. The purpose of this engagement is to participate in God's work of renewal in both individual and public life. Such historically redemptive action requires engaging forces of disharmony, dysfunctionality, and brokenness that operate at cross-purposes with God's will for human community in the social, political, and economic structures of society. Thus, while the Christian must ponder personal choices and interpersonal relationships, he or she must also challenge corporate decisions and agendas, including the government's, relative to how these affect the freedom, justice, prosperity, and pursuit of happiness of every person. The faith community cannot hope to remain faithful to the biblical witness if it interprets its social responsibility as an option rather than an inescapable mandate.

The invitational dilemma poses the problem of whether to interpret social and political engagement as a central or peripheral component of the divine call. The scriptural warrant, however, is clear: Christians are ambassadors for Christ, continuing his work of reconciliation in the world, redeeming both individuals and society. Thus a proper resolution of the invitational dilemma will contain responses that move beyond the immediate boundaries of self and church, and acknowledge the world as the sphere of discipleship activity.

An intimate encounter with the unfolding biblical narrative opens the reader to an emergent, progressive revelation. The disciple gradually discovers that despite God's rather intense love affair with Israel in the Old Testament and with the early church of the New, the world is ultimately the primary object of God's affection. Abraham's call in Genesis 12:1–4 lays the foundation for a universal, moral vision linked specifically to a salvation multinational in its concrete, historical expression. "Now the LORD said to Abram, 'Go from your country and your kindred and your father's house to the land that I will show you. I will make of you a great nation, and I will bless you, and make your name great, so that you will be a blessing. I will bless those who bless you, and the one who curses you I will curse; and in you all the families of the earth shall be blessed.' So Abram went, as the LORD had told him; and Lot went with him. Abram was seventy-five years old when he departed from Haran." The prophetic literature proclaims Israel "a light to the nations" (Isa. 49:6). God's election (invitational call) of Israel is intended not to establish its national superiority and geopolitical dominance, but rather to make Israel a conduit for cosmic redemption. Likewise, God's adoption of the followers of Christ in the New Testament must be seen in the light of Jesus' words to his disciples after the incident with the mother of the sons of Zebedee: "But Jesus called them to him and said, 'You know that the rulers of the Gentiles lord it over them, and their great ones are tyrants over them. It will not be so among you; but whoever wishes to be great among you must be your servant, and whoever wishes to be first among you must be your slave; just as the Son of Man came not to be served but to serve, and to give his life a ransom for many'" (Matt. 20:25–28). In the scriptural drama God's will for redemption extends to the entire world. Jesus Christ is Sovereign Lord of all. The call of God to the disciple in the gathered community, therefore, has implications far beyond the church itself.

As the object of God's love and care, the world is the theater of God's liberating and transforming work. Reconciling the world (which includes the church) into a proper fellowship is God's continuing goal. God works in and through people, places, events, and institutions of the world to effect God's redeeming purposes. The exodus and Jesus events demonstrate God's willingness to become involved in the world's thorny social and political realities. God never rejects the world or erases it from the divine agenda. God's back is never turned on the world. The call of God invites the disciple and the church to assume responsibility for the care of the world. This large task includes not just tree hugging but a concern for economic viability as well as sustainable environmental health. Many corporations are looking for people with so-called green MBAs, which include business acumen as well as sound environmental knowledge. The task also includes creative ways of dealing with immigration that avoid blatant racism and simplistic, unworkable solutions. The solution to the problem of illegal immigration is as human as it is legal. Essential fairness applies to immigrants, employers, ordinary taxpayers, governments of the countries of origin, to name a few. Dealing with national security and the threat of terrorism raises profound questions about the relationship between personal rights of privacy and our corporate need to be safe. Such discussions get at the heart of who we are as a people, let alone as Christians. These and many like issues are part of what it means to care about the stewardship of society.

A Plea for Engaged Piety

What difference does all of this make for the gathered community and the individual disciple? The answer to this question raises the issue of how we shall understand piety. The call of God is an invitation to participate in a new reality. A person is moved to focus on the things of God. A radical shift in the individual's interests may occur, based on an interpretation of Scripture and God's will for us as individuals and society. Persons who participate in this experience of renewal usually seek a deeper, closer relationship with God so that they might be better equipped to live a life of faithfulness to God's call. Piety is thus the form or pattern that this new orientation takes.

Piety means different things to different people. Some used it pejoratively to refer to stuffy religiosity, stiff-necked, puritanical, and goody-goody. But in a more general sense, it refers to the orientation of principles and actions possessed by everyone. In its religious form, it is simply the way the believer represents his or her reverence toward God through his or her actions in the world. The different forms of piety arise out of different interpretations of God, Scripture, and Jesus Christ. In this book I argue for a piety that is engaged in confronting the injustices of society for the purposes of transformation in contrast to a piety that is disengaged from such confrontation and transformation.

Engaged piety refers to a particular orientation toward reality fueled by a belief in and a commitment to the reality of God's sovereign and providential presence in the world. All piety combines reverence and love for God and a desire to know God properly in order to discern God's will for one's life, with a commitment to practice those disciplines that will enhance spiritual formation.[2] Piety does not occur automatically in a disciple upon answering the call of God but develops gradually and progressively through instruction, prayer, worship, and discernment. It must be intentionally nurtured through continual spiritual disciplines, which illustrates the importance of the community and its ethos in the process. The sustained ethos of the community can orient disciples toward an entirely private, interiorized, contemplative piety or toward a piety that links reverence to God with active engagement with the world for the sake of justice and peace.

Pietism was a movement in the Lutheran Church originated by Philipp Jakob Spener and lasting from the late seventeenth century to the mid-eighteenth century. It influenced John Wesley to begin the Methodist movement in England and the first Great Awakening in the new American colonies. Its influence is still with us. Prior to Spener, the Lutheran Church had become highly dogmatic and doctrinaire. Christianity consisted mainly in correctness of doctrine. It generated a "head" piety, cool, rational, creedal. Luther had placed Christianity in the heart, but those who followed him, such as Melanchthon, tried to construct the evangelical faith as a doctrinaire system and place it in the cool regions of the intellect. Dogmatic formularies of the Lutheran Church usurped the place Luther had given to the Bible alone.

To combat this trend, Spener combined Lutheran emphasis on biblical doctrine with Calvin's concern for the formulation of the Christian life. Knowledge of religion must be combined with religious practice. Sermons on Scripture must be practical and devotional rather than doctrinaire and legalistic. Christianity consists mainly in a change of heart and consequent holiness of life expressed in personal, moral purity. New birth brings a separation from the world so that one can practice personal holiness. For the Puritans in New England, this meant no dancing, card playing, or public, frivolous games.

Whatever the value of Spener's corrective to a church piety that had become detached from heart and emotion, one can see how it could lead to a piety equally detached from involvement in the struggle for justice and peace in society and world. All might agree that religious knowledge must be accompanied by related action, but how should such action be conceived, internally or externally? Or some combination of both? The virtue of pietism is that it engaged the heart; the disadvantage is that it tended to disengage the believer from God's work of transforming unjust and evil structures of society. The issue is twofold in this regard. To what extent is the individual believer called to engage in social transformation? And to what extent is the community of believers, the church, called to unmask corporate evil in the public square? Churches following in this tradition, relying heavily on the method of evangelical revivalism, understood piety primarily as a matter of personal conversion and the renewal of inward, spiritual affections. Hence they tended to focus on cultivating the inner religious life, emphasizing the individual's personal experience of Jesus and the Holy Spirit in the private, interior reaches of the soul.[3] The development of piety in these traditions remained fixated on redemption in the private sphere, aiming at changes in the lifestyles of individuals. Little attention was given to redemption in public life, and virtually no acknowledgment of the sin and evil operating in the powerful corporate structures of the social order. This piety tends to promote a dichotomy between the public and private dimensions of human life that contemporary churches are handling in different and unexpected ways.

The Bible contains clear mandates to join God in the struggle against evil and in the establishment of righteousness in the world. For some faith communities, an active engagement with the powerful social, political, and economic forces that work at cross-purposes with the divine will for the human community is an indispensable component of discipleship. To be a disciple is to be engaged with the full scope of human existence, including its concrete social and political dimensions. James says: "What good is it, my brothers and sisters, if you say you have faith but do not have works? Can faith save you? If a brother or sister is naked and lacks daily food, and one of you says to them, 'Go in peace, keep warm and eat your fill,' and yet you do not supply their bodily needs, what is the good of that? So faith by itself, if it has no works, is dead" (Jas. 2:14–17). Completeness in the faith requires complementary action.

True discipleship accepts its responsibility to share God's loving and gracious deeds with the human community. The disciple embraces his or her call to act as God's steward in the world. An engaged piety understands the necessity of personal spiritual conversion and growth, and structures programmatic life to meet these goals. However, an engaged piety understands that attention to individual empowerment is but one aspect in the dynamic of inner change and outward action. Therefore, an engaged piety rejects any tendency to focus its energies inwardly to the exclusion of the needs of the immediate social context. It denies any dualism of public/private, temporal/spiritual, personal/ social, individual/corporate.

An engaged piety involves itself in both short-term remedies to meet individual human needs and the analysis and addressing of the systemic, structural nature of social issues and ills. It understands that the issues of poverty, racism, sexism, violence, abuse, unemployment, and drug addiction, to name a few, are symptomatic effects of deeper, underlying maladies. Personal existence occurs within a broader social context. The existential plight of individuals cannot be separated from the social, political, economic, and just plain human matrices that hold them. Engaged piety knows that attempts to remedy personal misery without simultaneously addressing the sociocultural ethos and the institutional forces that operate to create that misery are inadequate and even morally irresponsible.

A church with an engaged piety links the nurturing activities of its inner life to its felt responsibility to remain socially and politically active in the world. Its internal life of celebration in worship, preaching, teaching, and equipping disciples in the spiritual disciplines of prayer and meditation is inseparable from its advocacy for just public policy and social institutions. Issues of economic justice, sexism, homophobia, and structural violence are as high on the prayer list as praying for the sick and the growth of the Sunday school. At stake is a commitment to a piety true to both the private and the public demands of biblical faith.

In short, a piety (reverence for God) that becomes disconnected from working for justice in the world renders one's faith inauthentic. Engaged piety is one in which the commitment to the practice of spiritual disciplines (prayer, fasting, etc.) is linked with a felt responsibility for the public order, which responsibility some consider a spiritual discipline. Disengaged piety is one in which this linkage does not occur.

The Presbyterian Church (U.S.A.) affirms the promotion of social righteousness and the exhibition of the kingdom of heaven to the world as two of the six great ends of the church.[4] It links these ends to one of the main themes of its historic tradition, namely, the sovereignty of God. In confessing God's sovereignty over all the created order, it sees itself as a community called into existence by God, and known to others in the world by both its convictions and its actions. Therefore, the Presbyterian Church (U.S.A.) interprets its calling as one that points beyond its own institutional concerns to its role as a sign in and for the world of the new reality that God has inaugurated in Jesus Christ. Therefore, its ethos sustains and promotes the important mandate not only to minister to the needs of individuals within its fellowship, but also to participate in God's redeeming activity in the world, engaging in the struggle against injustice and working for the establishment of Christ's rule of love, justice, and peace in society.[5]

Speaking in the specific context of racial oppression and discrimination in the United States in 1967, the Presbyterian Church (U.S.A.) not only confessed its involvement in the sin of racism, but also challenged itself to engage proactively in a ministry of reconciliation to include concrete witness, obedient action against racism, and the reconstruction of those interpersonal and institutional relationships that are contrary to God's will for the human community.[6]

At its General Assembly in Fort Worth, Texas, in June 1999, the Presbyterian Church (U.S.A.) unanimously adopted a policy document that set forth its intention not only to become an antiracist church, but also to work toward an antifascist society.[7] This is an example of one way a particular church family, in its written expression at least, tried to take seriously the emphasis of both personal nurture in the faith community and a sense of shared responsibility to be socially and politically involved in the world.

Without question, both the individual disciple and the church have to live in the world, within the fractured human community, not apart and protected from it. Thus an authentic encounter with God results in both inner, personal transformation and outer, public redemption. The redemptive community engages sin and evil not only in personal lives, but in corporate, institutional structures of society as well. Thus disciples look for more than projects directed solely at individual religiosity. Every disciple yearns for an intimate encounter with the risen Lord. It may be easier and safer to focus inordinately on individual experiences of grace, forgiveness, and personal growth, and it may be wiser economically to focus on such personal issues and soft-pedal social concerns. But God's gracious actions in the lives of solitary persons can never be separated from what God is doing in the structures of society. Therefore, a concern with corporate, communal renewal is always an integral component of spiritual development.

The church and individual disciples responding to the call of God have a responsibility for continual reexamination of social, political, and economic realities in light of the church's primary message of faith, hope, and love. It is this message that sustains disciples and generates within them dissatisfaction with the current brokenness in the world. The rhythm of discipleship does not allow praise of God, evangelistic focusing on winning souls for Christ, or a concentration on salvation from sin in personal lives to eclipse a disciple's concern about poverty, sexism, racism, or economic and political injustice. At the very core of discipleship is a call to engage the society and work toward the establishment of God's righteousness in the social and political order. The church is forever challenged to decide whether it will be content to serve merely as an empty symbol of God's loving and redeeming presence, or offer itself as a dynamic instrument of God's power to effect social as well as personal liberation in the world.

To reiterate: call and response occur within a community. The call comes through the community of faith; the response is lived out in the community of faith and into the world. The sacraments enact the gospel and the drama of call and response. Each is an activity of the community; each enacts the grace by which we are joined to Christ, united with him in his birth, life, death, and resurrection, confirming in us that "in Christ God was reconciling the world to himself, not counting their trespasses against them, and entrusting the message of reconciliation to us" so that "we are ambassadors for Christ" (2 Cor. 5:19–20).

3

What the Bible Says

*Call and Response in the Old Testament
Story of Amos*

Context of the Biblical Prophetic Tradition

The point of departure for a serious consideration of the importance of social and political engagement to the Christian faith is,
of course, the Bible, which contains many stories of call and
response. In the Hebrew Scriptures the prophetic literature
graphically illustrates the inseparable linkage between the
rhythm of divine call and human response, on the one hand, and
the necessity for responsible social and political engagement in
the world, on the other hand.

The stories and messages of Abraham, Moses, Deborah,
Samuel, Elijah, Nathan, Isaiah, Ezekiel, Hosea, Amos, Jeremiah,
and other biblical prophets are among the most quoted passages
of the Bible. Who were these people? What was the purpose of
their witness? What was the content of their message? It will be
helpful to highlight some of the prominent features of the
prophetic tradition in order to gain a clearer picture of the ramifications of Amos's call, the major focus of this chapter.

As a tradition of human response, the history of prophecy spans
several centuries and involves many diverse personalities. Luke
lists Moses, one of Israel's greatest spiritual leaders, as a prototype
of the prophets (Acts 3:21–24). Prophets were involved in the con-
quest of the Promised Land (Deborah in Judg. 4:6–7, 9, 14) as well
as during the transition to the monarchy (Samuel in 1 Sam. 3:20;
7:6, 15). Further, prophets served as advisors to Israel's kings,
offering critiques of policy and advice on matters of national security (Gad, Nathan, Elijah, Elisha in 1, 2 Kings). The classical or

writing prophets lived approximately in the eighth to the sixth centuries BCE. The Assyrian rise to power after 750 BCE provided the context for the prophetic ministries of Amos, First Isaiah, Hosea, and Micah. The Babylonian threat provided the background for the work of Jeremiah and Ezekiel. As the Persian Empire began its rise in the sixth century BCE, the stage was set for the prophecies of Second Isaiah, Obadiah, Haggai, Zechariah, and Malachi. When the temple of Jerusalem was destroyed in 587 BCE, the subsequent exile and enslavement of Israel gave rise to the exilic and postexilic prophets, especially Second Isaiah, who offered an elegant interpretation of Israel's fall and future redemption.

The most important term for "prophet" in Hebrew, *nabi*, means "one who is called." The biblical tradition understands a prophet as one called by God to speak a word from God to the people. Prophets appear at several major points throughout Israel's history to guide the nation's activity in accordance with God's will expressed in the covenant that God established with the elect Jewish community. The covenantal relationship was crucial since it established Israel's national identity as the children of God. Israel was to remain faithful to this covenant, specifically through worship and reverence for Yahweh and the keeping of the law given by Yahweh at Sinai, thereby securing its destiny as recipient of God's promise of land and prosperity.

During periods of impending national crisis prophets appeared quite often, largely unrecognized by the people. Into this situation the prophets spoke a decisive word from God about the nature and cause of the current crisis and what must be done to remedy or rectify it. In most cases, the crisis issued from the disregard and violation of covenantal responsibilities. Indeed, the point of departure for the prophets was Israel's struggle to remain faithful to the covenant. A crucial test of Israel's fidelity to God lay in the configurations of power in all phases of Israel's corporate life: personal, interpersonal, social, political, economic, and spiritual.

Biblical Prophetic Utterance: The Divine Call to a Socially Conscious Spirituality

The prophets were, among other things, the social conscience of the people. Their purpose was primarily to reaffirm and reestablish the connection between the moral-spiritual and sociopolitical dimensions of human living. An understanding of religion that fused private and public, individual and corporate, sacred and secular domains characterized prophetic speech and behavior. They were seers, but they did much more than merely predict the future. The messages they delivered were designed to call Israel back to a proper sense of honor, reverence, and obedience to God. Proper honor of God was not simply a matter of correct ritual and ceremony in the worship life of the community. More crucial than correct ritual for the honor of God was just social relationships. The prophets pointed to both these responsibilities as marks of fidelity to the covenant, which stressed equally the moral-spiritual realm and the sociopolitical. The key watchwords for the prophets' stress on public morality became *mishpat* and *sedaqah*, both of which can be translated "righteousness" and "justice." Thus when the prophets spoke God's Word to the nation about a particular national crisis, they began with a critique of national moral-spiritual health, the social and political power relationships of the society. To know why the nation is experiencing its current crisis, says the prophet, look at the way the nation is unfaithful to the covenant relationship. The covenant in its entirety stresses right relationship with God through both proper worship and just social structures. National identity, covenantal fidelity, worship life, moral-spiritual health, and social justice were all knitted together in the perspective of the prophet.

The prophets, while speaking to a variety of contexts, shared certain key experiences. Many point to a call from God commissioning them to speak and act on God's behalf. Many received a particular word from God about a specific set of circumstances. This word came in various modes: visions, dreams, direct appearances from God. They interpreted their call as a mandate to speak God's word of truth to the people. This word often contained these elements: a call to remember God's past relationship with Israel; a critique of present conditions; reasons for the current crisis; a forecast of what will likely happen if current trends continue; a call for repentance, *metanoia*, and a change in communal behavior through a return to covenantal faithfulness; a prediction of either God's redemption if they do repent or God's judgment if they do not. In addition to acting on behalf of the people, often through the performance of miraculous works, the prophets were uncompromising moral barometers for the nation. In this sense, they linked God's judgment of Israel's present and God's vision for Israel's future to an analysis of the nation's commitment to show mercy to the poor and oppressed, and to practice justice in dealing with the downtrodden and disadvantaged.

The prophets spoke from within the covenant relationship that Yahweh had so painstakingly established with Israel. There could be no substantive relationship with God apart from the existence of a viable community. There could be no viable community apart from fidelity to the covenant. There could be no fidelity to the covenant where worship life is severed from social responsibility. Hence right relationship with God was possible, the prophets insisted, only as individuals promoted justice in the social order. Authentic faith is socially conscious, linked to the pressing social and political issues to which God, through the prophets, was speaking. The prophets remind us that we must hear God's word to us as it emerges from within, not outside of, the current human predicament. An intimate relationship with God is simply not possible without sufficient intentionality in establishing justice in the social and political arrangements of power in the community.

The prophets assert that the world is the theater for divine activity. When prophets say "Thus says the Lord" (e.g. Amos 1:3), they are pointing to what God demands. In so doing, the prophets are telling us what God is like, what God is concerned about, and what God is up to in the world. What follows, usually, is a statement about the human community, public indictment of moral apostasy followed by the details of covenantal brokenness and coming judgment. We see this pattern in Amos 1–2, Jeremiah 5:10–17, and Micah 1:5–7. This prophetic pattern acknowledges the inseparable link between divine sovereignty and human responsibility. The prophets insisted that the disclosure of God's displeasure with injustice included a call to the human community for repentance.

The biblical prophets were profoundly aware of the communal context of individual choice. They deplored the attempt to develop an individual piety apart from the social context. They ridiculed the approach to spiritual wholeness limited to essentially private morality and copious cultic practice. Micah said:

Alas for those who devise wickedness
   and evil deeds on their beds!
When the morning dawns, they perform it,
   because it is in their power.
They covet fields, and seize them;
   houses, and take them away;
they oppress householder and house,
   people and their inheritance.
Therefore thus says the LORD:
Now, I am devising against this family an evil
   from which you cannot remove your necks;
and you shall not walk haughtily,
   for it will be an evil time.

Mic. 2:1–3

About taking refuge in cultic practice, Amos said:

I hate, I despise your festivals,
   and I take no delight in your solemn assemblies.
Even though you offer me your burnt offerings and grain offerings,
   I will not accept them;
and the offerings of well-being of your fatted animals
   I will not look upon.
Take away from me the noise of your songs;
   I will not listen to the melody of your harps.
But let justice roll down like waters,
   and righteousness like an ever-flowing stream.

Amos 5:21–24

We must conclude that the struggle for personal righteousness cannot be limited to private morals and individual behavior but must include analysis and intervention in the corporate-institutional arrangements of society. The prophets established the primacy of the communal realm as the appropriate context for reestablishing right relationship with God. The prophets served warning: there could be no authentic divine-human encounter apart from a legitimate human-human interaction. The basis of legitimate human-human interaction was, of course, *sedaqah*, "justice."

The prophets refused to allow the faith community to believe that proper spiritual growth was possible apart from engagement with the social context. This entailed intentional, responsible participation in the structures of society as well as in individual interpersonal relationships. Such activity must be grounded in the moral-spiritual norms of righteousness and justice. Whenever the nation failed to give due regard to the ways in which it structured its human-human relationships, the prophets issued stern reminders of the disastrous consequences of this lapse.

The task of the prophet was to speak the divine imperative in the human situation. Micah says:

The voice of the LORD cries to the city
    (it is sound wisdom to fear your name):
Hear, O tribe and assembly of the city!
    Can I forget the treasures of wickedness in the house of the
        wicked, and the scant measure that is accursed?
Can I tolerate wicked scales
    and a bag of dishonest weights?
Your wealthy are full of violence;
    your inhabitants speak lies,
    with tongues of deceit in their mouths.

Mic. 6:9–12

The prophets zeroed in on the concrete practices of dishonest weights and crooked scales in the marketplace. They conveyed God's impatience with those who professed faith in God while remaining indifferent to God's demand for honesty and justice in the corporate life of the city. Religious ceremony and ritual could not substitute for the genuine righteousness of seeking justice and mercy.

The prophets heard God's call as a call to a socially conscious spirituality. This theme runs through all of the prophets, although in varying degrees. It is not until the rise of the later prophets, such as Jeremiah and Ezekiel, that we begin to witness even the faintest notion of individual salvation. Without question, in the majority of prophetic literature, the notion of an individual piety or a personal redemption nurtured apart from the community is absent. For the prophets, if the community is doomed, so is everyone else, even those faithfully striving to be in right relationship with God. God's judgment is corporate, taking the innocent along with the guilty, as Abraham's arguing with God over the fate of the few righteous in Sodom demonstrates (Gen. 18:22–33). For the prophets, although guilt may be avoided by some in the community, responsibility cannot. There is no individual salvation or sectarian redemption apart from the fate of the whole community.

Amos: The Promotion of Socially Responsible Faith

Amos is a clear example of socially conscious spirituality. He is the first of the literary prophets. He was a sheepherder and a dresser of sycamore trees (figs) in Tekoa, a village in the Judean hills about six miles south of Bethlehem, in approximately 760 BCE when God said to him, "Go, prophesy to my people Israel" (Amos 7:14–15). Although a citizen of southern Judah, his call sent him to the northern kingdom of Israel, which was under the rule of Jeroboam II. He thundered stern, moral critiques against Israel, Samaria, Bethel, and the power elites who ruled the land. His stinging indictments unmasked the glaring inconsistencies in the nation's public life. On one hand, prosperity existed for a select minority who enjoyed inordinate wealth, opulence, and a disproportionate access to power and control through their access to the palace structures. On the other hand, the poor suffered injustice, exploitation, and affliction in the marketplace and judicial system. Even the judges, those charged with guarding the rights of the public, were guilty of corruption, in some cases participating in the selling of the poor into slavery. The desire among the rich for continuing economic prosperity, which supported a decadent and luxurious lifestyle, combined with moral corruption and idolatry, had a devastating impact upon those who were without power, resources, or protection in the community.

Into this situation came the thunderous utterances of Amos. His public jeremiads against injustice in the society audaciously linked stern warnings of the nation's impending doom with a diagnosis of the moral state of Israel. Amos assessed that state of moral health in terms of the relative economic, social, and political justice present in Israel. His conclusion: how could a nation for whom God had provided such unparalleled privilege behave so contrary to the covenant they had made with God? Amos said, "The LORD roars from Zion, and utters his voice from Jerusalem" (1:2a); "the lion has roared, who will not fear? The Lord GOD has spoken; who can but prophesy?" (3:8). The message was that God roared like a lion against Israel's increasing unfaithfulness, sinfulness, and moral apostasy.

Amos also pronounced judgments against Israel's neighbors: Syria, Philistia, Phoenicia, Edom, Ammon, and Moab. By including the sins of the surrounding nations, Amos reminded Israel that the covenant Yahweh established with them was but a means to the greater end of effecting righteousness and justice in the whole world. The covenant that specified the nature of the relationship between Israel and Yahweh was meant to be a model for all the other nations of the world. National survival was linked to the social, political, and economic condition of each nation's citizens.

Amos's message made the comparison between Israel and the surrounding nations with brute honesty. It was one thing, said Amos, for nations who did not enjoy a covenantal relationship with God to behave in morally apostate and sinful ways. It was another matter altogether for a nation that did enjoy such a relationship to behave in ways equally sinful and immoral. Amos came to Judah and Israel (the southern and northern kingdoms of Israel) and issued a judgment against both for their morally shameful behavior. For their guilt, they too would feel the wrath of Yahweh's punishment, just as the surrounding nations would. Both kingdoms, Judah and Israel, would receive harsher judgment because they had enjoyed greater privilege and hence assumed greater moral culpability.

The most conspicuous example of Israel and Judah's culpability lay in their idolatrous approach to the covenantal relationship. God's election of Israel and Judah had privileged them to enjoy a special relationship with a God who had loved them in spite of their lowly position. Now, these people of the covenant had become misoriented, focusing on self-indulgence, polluted wealth, and vain and luxurious living. In a word, they had ceased to walk faithfully with God, and nowhere was this more apparent than in their idolatrous pollution of the altars of worship at the temple centers at Bethel, Gilgal, and Beersheba (cf. 5:4–5). The shrines and sanctuaries of Yahweh had been polluted with idols of other nations. Empty ceremonialism and profane ritualism replaced a genuine, covenantal relationship with Yahweh. Since Israel and Judah had failed to respond properly to Yahweh's mercy, justice, and love, Yahweh would judge them in justice, love, and wrath.

For Amos, the chief characteristic of this misplaced religion was the idolatrous immorality of the people while at the same time harboring a notion of divine favor. Amos debunked the popular misconception of the long-awaited Day of the Lord as a period of vindication against their enemies. Instead, he argued, because of their apostasy, idolatry, and injustice, this day would come to engulf them as a period of disaster and gloom. "Alas for you who desire the day of the LORD! Why do you want the day of the LORD? It is darkness, not light. . . . Is not the day of the LORD darkness, not light, and gloom with no brightness in it?" (5:18, 20). Amos delivered this devastating indictment not only against the ruler, Jeroboam II, but also in the very heart of the center of the worshiping community: against the priest, Amaziah, and the court prophets at the main sanctuary at Bethel (7:10–17).

The sum of the judgments against the nation, as well as of the visions of divine wrath (locust plagues, fruit basket, drought, plumb line, altar), was to make clear the causal relationship between polluted worship and social injustice and national calamity. What God really required, said Amos, was to "let justice roll down like waters, and righteousness like an ever-flowing stream" (5:24). Instead, the nation had not only desecrated the altars of worship with polluted idols, and substituted empty ritual for intimacy in the covenantal relationship, they had sought God's favor for this shameful behavior and had fooled themselves into believing that God had sanctioned it with divine approval. In this way, believing themselves immune from the threat of foreign enemies, and waiting expectantly for a total vindication in a future Day of the Lord, the people of God had failed to remember that their treatment of the least-advantaged members of the community was the true indication of moral health.

At the same time, the business elite engaged in dishonest practices resulting in heavy oppression of the poor. A lack of loyalty to the covenant was, therefore, paralleled by an equal lack of pity and compassion for the poor. Amos's stinging public indictments aimed at jolting the nation into the realization that fidelity to the covenant involved an acknowledgment of the inescapable connection between the worship of God and the practice of justice in the economic, social, and political relationships of the community.

Amos issued scathing denunciations of the nation's sinful religious and social practices, and warned of approaching national doom. The people who had once enjoyed a sanctified status, separated by God for special service in and to the world, had fallen into the same abominations and sins as the other nations. In their inability to extricate themselves from their predicament, they were headed for invasion by their enemies, exile, poverty, and, ultimately, national death. The remedy was to return to a proper walk with God. The nation's moral-spiritual disinterest in the injustices of the day would not go unpunished by a God who had demonstrated a pronounced divine interest in mercy and justice in the social order.

Amos put before Israel and Judah an alternative vision of the content of the divine-human relationship. Worship could not be reduced to mere ritual and ceremony, nor could worship serve as the sole means of identification for the chosen people of God. Amos envisioned a right relationship with God as twofold: the proper worship of God and the promotion of social justice in the community. Worship includes a genuine encounter with God. Authentic worship includes heeding God's call for justice.

The story of Amos is a model of the way in which the rhythm of call and response operates. God called Amos to speak God's word to Israel, to which Amos responded by thundering his oracles against Israel and its neighbors. That prophetic word was itself a divine invitation to Israel to become a light unto the nations, and an invitation not only to Israel but also to all the nations who make up the human community. It was a call to become proactively involved in God's work of establishing righteousness and justice in societal relationships and institutional arrangements. Amos linked faithfulness to God to justice in communal existence, a new riff in the melody line of spiritual faithfulness for his hearers, even though that note had always been part of the covenantal law. Amos gives us a God so interested in the moral-spiritual health of the community that God predicates proper divine-human relationship on attention to justice in social relationships. In a stirring warning, God says through Amos:

> Hear this word, you cows of Bashan
>   who are on Mount Samaria,
> who oppress the poor, who crush the needy,
>   who say to their husbands, "Bring something to drink!"
> The Lord GOD has sworn by his holiness:
>   The time is surely coming upon you,
> when they shall take you away with hooks,
>   even the last of you with fishhooks.
>
> Amos 4:1–2

To reiterate: spiritual faith requires engagement in the establishment of human communities that do not hypocritically feign endorsement of justice while tolerating or participating in injustice. Amos's prophetic witness points to the impossibility of attempts at spiritual formation that do not include an interest and investment in social and political realities. Virtually all the prophetic figures of the Old Testament include this theme. We turn, next, to an exploration of how the public ministry of Jesus reappropriates the prophetic message for a later era.

4

Call and Response
in the New Testament

The Life of Jesus

> *"The Spirit of the Lord is upon me,*
> *because he has anointed me*
> *to bring good news to the poor.*
> *He has sent me to proclaim release to the captives*
> *and recovery of sight to the blind,*
> *to let the oppressed go free,*
> *to proclaim the year of the Lord's favor."*
> Luke 4:18–19

*J*esus responded to God's call just as Amos and the other prophets of Israel had before him. He was faithful even unto death. Jesus exemplifies the truth that it is not just the fact of one's calling but how one responds that is of paramount importance. At an early age he exhibited his independence from all earthly authority, including that of his parents, in favor of allegiance to his divine calling. On one of the family's annual pilgrimages to Jerusalem for the Passover festival, the twelve-year-old Jesus remained behind without telling the family when they left for home. Upon discovering his absence, his parents returned to Jerusalem and searched for him for three days. When they found him in the temple, his mother took him to task for causing them so much anxiety. But he calmly replied, "Why were you searching for me? Did you not know that I must be in my Father's house?" (Luke 2:49). Responding to God's call eventually led Jesus into a protracted and dangerous confrontation with the religious authorities and their narrow interpretation of God's law. His response led him, eventually, to the cross.

Jesus: God-with-Us

In the economy of call and response, Jesus is both the model and the power. The incarnation assures us that union with Christ is possible. God was in Christ; we humans unite with Christ. We are related to Christ and, through him, to God. God was in Christ and thereby effects our redemption, our union with God, forgiving our sins and not counting our trespasses against us. Jesus does not have a relationship with God; he is God incarnate. At the same time, "we do not have a high priest who is unable to sympathize with our weaknesses, but we have one who in every respect has been tested as we are, yet without sin" (Heb. 4:15). We sit with Christ at the banquet table of the called. He is like us in every way, save his being without sin. He is also quite unique, "for in him all the fullness of God was pleased to dwell, and through him God was pleased to reconcile to himself all things, whether on earth or in heaven, by making peace through the blood of his cross" (Col. 1:19–20). This fullness may be ours as well, as Paul implies when he says to the Ephesians, "I pray that you might have the power . . . to know the love of Christ that surpasses knowledge, so that you may be filled with all the fullness of God" (Eph. 3:18–19).

Beginning with Paul and continuing to the present day, there has been a continuous effort to make sense of the identity, purpose, and relevance of Jesus for the church and the world. A host of christological debates, conferences, councils, position papers, and creedal statements dot the ecclesial landscape.[1] In recent decades liberationist, feminist, black, Asian, Hispanic, and African (to name a few) voices have joined the christological conversation.

While I believe that traditional christological formulations continue to have merit and must not be discounted, I also believe that we have to listen carefully to the new voices in the conversation that offer hard challenges to traditional christological perspectives. These "alternative voices" provide ways of understanding Jesus Christ that, while sometimes disconcerting, highlight the proactive aspect of Christology. The traditional voices focused more on the theoretical and personal dimensions of Jesus' meaning and relevance. Hence the concern was correct belief or orthodoxy. The new voices tend to lift up the practical and communal dimensions of Jesus' meaning and relevance. The concern is primarily right action or orthopraxy. When heard together, these orthodoxy and orthopraxy orientations provide a truer and more usable Christology in the sense that the activist dimension in Christology is not diluted or eliminated entirely.

Christians are right to proclaim Jesus unashamedly and unapologetically as the Christ, the unique incarnation of God in the world and in human history. Indeed, Jesus ought to be recognized as the preeminent head of the community of faithful Christian believers, the church, proclaimed Savior and Lord by the power of the Holy Spirit. In Jesus the Christ, God has acted definitively in the world to reconcile the world to God's own Self. As such, God, through Jesus the Christ, calls the church into being, nurtures and equips disciples for service in the world to establish and extend the reign of God's kingdom.[2] As the church proclaims this good news, however, it must still ask: What does all of this mean? What does Jesus the Christ have to do with the human condition manifested in the particular contexts of brokenness, distorted relationships, massive poverty and hunger; of the divisive madness of racism, sexism, classism, violence, war, and abuse; of the psychic dislocation of apathy and despair?

Jesus as Organic Spiritualist

The distinction between the Jesus of history and the Christ of faith has been a major concern for the Jesus Seminar, founded by Robert Funk. This group of biblical scholars meets regularly to assess the authenticity of the words and acts of Jesus in the Gospels. They attempt to differentiate between the portrait of Jesus in the Gospels as a historical figure prior to his death (the pre-Easter Jesus of history) and what the church's developing tradition has said about him after his death (the post-Easter Jesus or Christ of faith). These scholars recognize that the Gospel writers were not disinterested social commentators or historians. Hence they argue that the Gospels cannot be approached as if they are narratives of hard, objective, historical facts.[3] Rather, the Gospels contain a mixture of both fact and embellishment designed to promote a certain theological perspective about God's ways with the world through Jesus. Hence scholars raise critical issues with the

Gospel texts as they try to ascertain what Jesus *actually* said and did as opposed to what the writer *claims* he said and did. Some of the conclusions reached by the Jesus Seminar have been explosive and shocking to people both inside and outside the church. I am not an apologist for this perspective, but I believe that some of the insights are highly relevant to any discussion of the meaning of Jesus for us today. The important issues, I believe, relate to what the Gospel narratives tell us about God's relationship to the world, and how the narratives become morally compelling for the community of faith in its response to what God is doing in, to, and with the world.

As a member of the post-Easter Jesus community, I think that the "profile" or "sketch" of the pre-Easter Jesus offered by Marcus Borg of the Jesus Seminar provides a helpful way of understanding the socio-political impact of Jesus' ministry. Borg offers four elements in his discussion of the pre-Easter Jesus: (1) "A spirit person"—one of a group of human personalities in history who have a unique God-consciousness and, through deeper and sustained communion with the Divine, experience a heightened awareness of the Holy. (2) "A wisdom teacher"—a gifted storyteller, similar to African griots who expertly utilize the forms of classic storytelling such as parables and short phrases to dispense "subversive" or "alternative" wisdom. This is juxtaposed to "conventional" wisdom that promotes an inordinate internalization of and conformity to the values, presuppositions, and objectives of the mainstream, status-quo culture. (3) "A social prophet"—linked to the tradition of prophetic utterance and witness exhibited by the classical prophets of ancient Israel. In this sense Jesus articulated an alternative religious and social vision that was often opposed to the religious and political elites of his time. (4) "A movement founder"—a religious organizer who was a primary architect and leader of a radical renewal of both religious and social communities. Jesus, in this view, talked and lived in such a way that his very presence shattered previously held spiritual notions and societal norms and customs.[4]

These four elements taken together provide, I believe, a powerful insight into the meaning and relevance of Jesus as the Christ, attested in Scriptures and affirmed by the church. Combined, these elements portray Jesus the Christ as an organic spiritualist. They emphasize the two primary spiritual axes around which the heart of Christian faith revolves: love of God and love of neighbor (Mark 12:28–31). In high-lighting the relational aspect of spiritual formation, Jesus' life, teach-ings, and ministry establish the linkage between God-consciousness and active involvement in the human community. By "organic spiri-tualist," I mean: (1) one who operates out of a sense of "call," that is, with the conviction that God has enlisted one in a cause that is larger than oneself, and with the understanding that God expects one to per-form some special task vital to the accomplishment of that divine plan. Organic spiritualists radically surrender and to obey what they discern as the will of God in the human situation. (2) One who links the expe-rience of spiritual consciousness to concrete witness in the world, to the idea that God is up to something radically transformative in the world, some unique vision compelling in its fundamental difference from present realities. This spiritual awareness is a gift which brings with it a great responsibility to become actively engaged in God's work of transformation. In this spiritual awareness, the active life of the mind and the practice of spiritual disciplines have social-moral ends. (3) One who practices risky modes of living, thinking, speak-ing, being, and acting in accordance with the radical divine vision. This lifestyle spawns active engagement with both individuals and systems that is often confrontational due to the opposing value sys-tem it promotes. Hence the organic spiritualist is often perceived as a threat to the established order and risks loss of prestige, security, and even life. Together, these three foci point to the organic spiritualist as one who links the development of spiritual awareness (relationship with God) to proactive engagement with the world, aiming at the transformation of human personalities (moral and psychic dimen-sions) and corporate institutions (social, political, economic dimen-sions) in accordance with an alternative vision.

In the Gospel narratives we learn about the call of God on Jesus' own life (see Matt. 4:1–11; Mark 1:9–13; Luke 4:16–30). In his teach-ing and parables, Jesus links seeking a right relationship with God to seeking right relationship with others in one's daily life (see Matt. 25:31–46). Jesus promoted a radically different faith perspective and corresponding ethic that proved unpalatable to the religious and cul-tural elites. Eating with sinners, healing on the Sabbath, forgiving the adulterous woman, each was an affront to the self-righteous legal purists of his time. His vision of what God required spawned a scathing public critique of the religious and social order reminiscent of the prophetic tradition of Amos, Isaiah, Hosea, Ezekiel, and others. Jesus' radical promotion of this vision landed him in turbulent waters and at odds with the powerful, who saw him as a distinct threat to their own arrangements of power.

The organic spirituality of Jesus did not permit any permanent withdrawal from the world into a shell of strictly personal piety. Jesus counseled against ostentatious prayer, urging people not to "be like the hypocrites; for they love to stand and pray in the synagogues and at the street corners" but instead to "go into your room and shut the door" (Matt. 6:5a, 6a). He never counseled people to stay in their room. In Jesus the community of Christian disciples sees what it really means to make a faithful response to the call of a God who is actively working in human affairs to liberate, redeem, and reconcile a broken community. In Jesus personal salvation and social transformation become two sides of the same coin. Jesus shows us that an authentic life under the conditions of human brokenness cannot separate love of God and love of neighbor. The call to a life of communion with God is essentially a relational rather than a conceptual matter. Saying yes to the call of God initiates the development of a spiritual consciousness that embraces with equal power both the personal and sociopolitical aspects of one's life. Jesus made this abundantly clear at the beginning of his ministry when, in the synagogue at Nazareth, he read from the scroll of Isaiah:

> "The Spirit of the Lord is upon me,
>   because he has anointed me
>   to bring good news to the poor.
> He has sent me to proclaim release to the captives
>   and recovery of sight to the blind,
>   to let the oppressed go free,
> to proclaim the year of the Lord's favor."
>
> Luke 4:18–19

When he finished, he said, "Today this scripture has been fulfilled in your hearing" (v. 21). This is how he understood his ministry.

In both his life and his teaching, Jesus models a personal piety that includes a deep concern for the welfare of the "other," the neighbor.

His concern for "lost" individuals extends to both physical and spiritual needs. He told Peter, "Feed my sheep" (John 21:17), and to all of the disciples he said, "Do not let your hearts be troubled. Believe in God, believe also in me" (John 14:1). At the beginning of his ministry, Jesus intentionally broke with established tradition and headed for the centers of urban blight where prostitutes, sinners, publicans, lepers, and other outcasts had to live. His proactive involvement in the lives of these people indicates his complete identification with the poor, the oppressed, the sick, and the lonely.

His affection for such people is clear from the Gospel text. What may be less clear is how Jesus' organic spirituality extends the love ethic beyond mere personal sympathy and care to the more radical idea of transforming the social order through the coming of the kingdom of God. The reign of God includes a particular vision for the social, political, and economic relationships of the human community. The conversion experience and subsequent spiritual formation might begin as an interior, personal, and even private experience; it certainly does not end there. By the power of the Holy Spirit, what may begin as an interior happening between the individual disciple and God moves outside to the community of the faithful and into the world of human affairs where the values of love, justice, and peace are applied to the corporate systems, institutions, and structures that heavily impact and shape individual human existence. Jesus aimed at fundamentally altering the social, political, and economic landscape.

Of course, at no point does the Jesus of the Scriptures offer a concrete program analogous to capitalism, socialism, democracy, oligarchy, or any other such form. Jesus' vision, however, did present a value system opposed to the prevailing conventions. He found the business-as-usual approach then current in the commercial, religious, and political realms totally inadequate and unacceptable. Because he threatened the established order, religious and political authorities feared him. It was not because of Jesus' kindness toward broken and lost people and the clever parables he told that led the authorities to condemn him. Rather, it was because his public moral and social vision challenged their whole social order. Jesus' vision presented such a radical alternative to the prevailing ethos that Jesus had to be either co-opted or destroyed. From the very beginning, Jesus' presentation of his message left little doubt as to his ultimate fate. Jesus could not avoid confrontation with the powerful social and political forces. Though tempted by the devil to take a different, and perhaps an easier, way (Matt. 4:1–11), he rejected the devil and marched on toward the cross.

All of this has profound ramifications for those called to be organic spiritualists. Jesus' focus on love of neighbor is rooted in the prophetic tradition of Amos and Micah that exhibits such great concern for peace and justice in the community. Jesus expressed this concern for public health in his preaching, teaching, and healing ministries. Like the prophets of old, he railed against the public institutions that exploited, victimized, and disempowered the poor, the outcast, and the stranger.

Table Connections in the Drama of Call and Response

Gathering at my family dinner table always reminds me of the way the Christian community gathers at the Lord's Table. Like my family, the church has its own special table where the entire extended family of Christ's disciples periodically gathers to reaffirm its commitment to the lordship of Jesus the Christ. Ingesting the spiritual food of Christ's body and blood, we participate in Christ's life, death, and resurrection. In this way the church's future hope of cosmic resurrection is linked inseparably to a shared past. What God has done in the past, God is also doing now in the present, and will do in the future. The community remembers, celebrates, and participates in Jesus' call. What God's call required in the past is likewise required in the present. The community rededicates itself to carry out its own call in the contemporary situation.[5]

The invitation to the Lord's Table includes a reminder that along with participating in Christ's death and resurrection, the disciple is recommitting him- or herself to a life of active engagement and service in the world. Holy Communion is where the church witnesses to God's act in our creation as a church and publicly acknowledges its call and mandate for responsible participation in God's ongoing work of redemption in human history. In this way we recognize the Jesus of history as the Christ of faith, and this presence at the table resurrects, revitalizes, and transforms the gathering into the new community of organic spiritualists.

The Christian community proclaims Jesus' life to be an event decisive for the history of the world. This is not merely the story of another heroic figure who stood up to the power structures of his time but was crushed by them. The proclamation of the gospel demands a choice, either for or against its claim: "Now after John was arrested, Jesus came to Galilee, proclaiming the good news of God, and saying, 'The time is fulfilled, and the kingdom of God has come near; repent, and believe in the good news'" (Mark 1:14–15). Not to decide is to decide. There is no middle ground. In its assent to the truth of the narrative, the church lives its life as the chanticleer of the kingdom of God. The narrative not only has salvific meaning but also decisively directs how the resident community of organic spiritualists organize their corporate life together as well as how they relate to the world. For the believer, then, participation in Christ's presence at the table mandates a responsible participation in the church, community, and world. Thus "apathetic, uninvolved Christian" is an oxymoron, since there is really no way to be a Christian disciple apart from active engagement with the powerful social, economic, and political forces at work in the world. This is what it means to speak of responding to God's vocational call. And remember the context of this participation: the Lord's Table, that is, within the community of the called. We do not speak here of solitary individuals sent out to tilt at windmills but of the company of the committed, a body of believers, who respond to God's call in Christ together in worship, sacrifice, and works of love, charity, and justice in the world in Christ's name.

At the table of our Lord the drama of call and response is enacted. Our decision to come to the table and be a part of the community is, at the same time, a choice to join God's work of liberation and reconciliation in the world. We are table people. Throughout history, ordinary individuals have accepted this invitation and responded to God's call with extraordinary results. Their decision has inevitably led to engagement with the sociopolitics of their time. It is to one of these organic spiritualists that we now turn, as we look to the city of Geneva, Switzerland.

Call and Response
in the Reformed Tradition

Calvin in Geneva

Faith by itself cannot please [God], since without love of neighbor there is no faith. . . . Love of God must be joined with love of neighbor.[1]

Not that love of neighbor is more important than the service to God, but that men can prove their loyalty to God only by living honestly and doing no injury to their neighbors. By the words justice *and* right judgment, *[the prophet] includes the kind of equity which gives to each man his due. . . .* Justice *implies the honesty and kindness which we practice, when we strive to help our brothers in every way and avoid hurting them in any way by fraud and violence.* Right judgment *means that we stretch out our hands to the poor and oppressed, that we see and support good causes, that we work hard to keep the weak from being unjustly hurt. These are the lawful tasks with which the Lord orders his own to keep occupied.*[2]

The Call to Organic Spirituality in Geneva

Alister E. McGrath ranks John Calvin (1509–1564) as one of those few, seminal figures, such as Marx and Lenin, whose life and thought directly molded the history of their time. "The ideas, outlook and structures developed by Calvin proved capable of generating and sustaining a movement which transcended the limitation of his historical location and personal characteristics."[3] He was, McGrath says, a religious thinker and a theologian but with important differences.

To describe him as a theologian is proper but misleading, given the modern associations of the term. A theologian is now one who is generally seen to be marginalized as an irrelevance by church and academy alike, whose public is limited to a severely restricted circle of fellow theologians, and whose ideas and methods are generally derived from other intellectual disciplines. The originality, power and influence of Calvin's religious ideas forbid us to speak of him merely as a "theologian"—though he certainly was—in much the same way as it is inadequate to refer to Lenin as a mere political theorist. Through his remarkable ability to master languages, media and ideas, his insights into the importance of organization and social structures, and his intuitive grasp of the religious needs and possibilities of his era, Calvin was able to forge an alliance between religious thought and action which made Calvinism a wonder of its age.[4]

Calvin ranks as one of the most recognizable names in the history of Christianity. His thought has provided the basis for centuries of theological formulation. It has also served as a major influence on social and political philosophies throughout the world. Calvin's influence extends beyond the Geneva of the sixteenth century to France, the United States, England, and South Africa, to name a few, and to historical movements such as the Puritans and the Scots. Calvin's views on God, human nature, the Bible, the church, the Christian life, and civil government have been studied, challenged, debunked, and appropriated by countless citizens, politicians, religious specialists, and social reformers. Some have agreed, some have opposed, but few have ignored him. Indeed, even the twentieth-century American prophet of social reform Martin Luther King Jr. had to consider the impact of Calvin's thought in light of the black-led, 1950–1960s modern civil rights movement. In the same vein, Allan Boesak's involvement in the movement to resist and dismantle racial apartheid in the South African context of the 1980–1990s felt the need to engage in critical dialogue with Calvin and his legacy.[5] Given this résumé, one might be surprised, as assuredly were the residents of sixteenth-century Geneva, to come across this preeminent theologian of the Reformation prowling about the sewers of the city. But he did just that, for he was concerned for the health of the town's citizens and considered no aspect of life beyond the ken of God's inquisitive, caring scrutiny, even the sewers of Geneva.

Calvin would hardly have predicted all of this for himself. In fact, he sought the obscure, serene, and austere life of a simple lawyer. Calvin claimed that only God could have taken him from his humble beginnings and honored him with the high office of minister of the gospel. Calvin was born in 1509 about sixty miles from Paris. At age fourteen his father sent him to further his education in Paris, where he excelled in his studies. His father had originally intended him to study philosophy and theology, but later, in 1528, enrolled him in a program of legal study at Orléans. After his father's death in 1531, he returned to Paris to immerse himself in a study of the ancient classics, and in 1532 published a monumental commentary on the *De Clementia* of Seneca. By the leading of God's providence, he says, his life was again redirected back to the church. While in Paris, in 1533, he underwent what he called a "sudden conversion," though historians debate how "sudden" it was. Nevertheless, with a zeal for "true religion" he decided, in 1534, to renounce Romanism and convert to Protestantism. Immediately, he left France to pursue a course of life he had outlined for himself. Settling in Basel, he published the first edition of the *Institutes of the Christian Religion* in 1536, at age twenty-six, which went on to become one of the most famous and influential books in history.

Following the publication of the *Institutes*, Calvin sought to travel to Strasbourg to devote himself to a life of study. His intentions were to stop at Geneva for one day, and then proceed on his journey. He said that he was by nature a man of the country and a lover of shade and leisure who wanted to retreat to a quiet life of obscurity and leisure. As it turned out, says Calvin, "God had stretched forth His hand upon me from on high to arrest me."[6] William Farel, a local minister who had come to Geneva in 1532, was active in converting the city to reformist ideas and in establishing Protestantism as the foundation for both private citizenship and public policy. Farel was the instrument by which God's call on Calvin's life was delivered. Farel needed an energetic organizer, a person with administrative gifts to help him with the task of corporate conversion. He appealed to Calvin to remain in Geneva and to assist in organizing the church, and he would not take no for an answer. By Calvin's own account, Farel terrorized him into involvement. Thus, believing he had indeed heard the divine call, Calvin stayed in Geneva and threw himself, along with Farel, into ecclesial reform.[7] As it turned out, it was a call to what I have referred to as "organic spirituality."

The initial call appeared limited to the institutional church. The context of Calvin's work was the contentious political dynamics of medieval church reformation, brewing since the thirteenth century and bursting into flames in the fifteenth century. The issues included institutional decadence, corruption, and immorality. The compromising of church doctrine and practice with secular ideologies and agendas, blatantly unfair taxation of church members, and rampant clerical abuses and scandals expressed through a variety of contemptible activities (e.g., simony, nepotism, indulgences, superstitions, lack of education, absenteeism) were all ingredients of a bad situation. The immensely wealthy medieval church had begun to lose its soul to material greed and lust for power. In this climate one might have expected people to give up completely on the church.

The age, however, was permeated by the religious spirit, and the forerunners of the Reformation sought to bring about badly needed change in the church. The conciliar movement of the early 1400s attempted to reform the church, root out heretical views, and provide ecclesial organization. The mystics of the mid- to late 1400s, represented by thinkers like Thomas à Kempis, sought to reform the church by placing greater emphasis on the inwardness of religion. Hence spiritual formation stressed piety as a mystical experience, a function of the inner, contemplative life. Although the mystics did stress service to the needy as an aspect of life in Christ, private, interior spirituality was the essential core of their approach. Building upon the foundations laid by the conciliarists and the mystics, individual reformist thinkers arose in various countries to advance the cause of change: John Wycliffe in England, the martyr John Hus of Bohemia, and the martyr Savonarola in Florence.

Yet, perhaps the most controversial group of Reformation predecessors were the humanists, represented by Erasmus of Rotterdam. The humanists' valorization of human reason led to the view that the church could be reformed from within by seeking the liberation of its members from the clutches of stagnating dogma. The route to salvation for individual and church was through, in a word, enlightenment. Stressing the self-sufficiency and goodness of the human, the humanists sought to reform the church by dispelling ignorance. If humans could somehow come to know the good, humans would more probably choose to do the good. Hence the humanists were influential for later Reformers like Luther, Zwingli, Bucer, and Farel in preparing the soil for change through promotion of humanist ideas such as the need for education and the stress on inward piety. In addition, the humanists' denunciation of the uselessness of externals in worship and their attack on corruption and vice in the church provided a foundation for courageous challenges to church authority. The Anabaptists at Zurich and Munster led by thinkers like Thomas Münzer, Berndt Knipperdolling, and Menno Simons also broke away from the Roman Church in the mid-1500s. Although their doctrine and practices were often in opposition to the ideas of first-generation Protestant Reformers like Luther in Germany and Zwingli in Zurich, they nevertheless pushed the Reformers to be true to the sense of public responsibility. Their stress on the practical, socio-ethical dimension of religion rather than doctrinal system was a healthy counterbalance to the inward, mystical dimension promoted by the mystics and humanists.[8]

Calvin: A Second-Generation Reformer

Calvin inherited a sociocultural milieu that had been thoroughly infused with an electric ethos of reformist ideas and practices. This dynamic atmosphere provided the cultural medium for Calvin's innovative linkage of spirituality and social reconstruction. Luther's break with Rome was a singular historical event, but the task of organizational refinement remained. As a professor of sacred learning, Calvin began to provide instruction in the faith and to develop a structure for authority and discipline in church matters. The moral reform of the church was the primary objective. The moral laxity of the church had leaked into home and marketplace and had a deleterious effect on the whole city of Geneva. Calvin, with Farel's support, turned his attention to the discipline of the entire city populace. He appointed a panel of church ministers and civil magistrates who drafted legislation regulating every public activity from dress codes and recreational activities to adultery and heresy. Delinquents were punished through pillory, arrest, banishment, or death. The two governing councils of Geneva, the Little Council of Twenty-five and the larger Council of Two Hundred, adopted Calvin's Twenty-one Articles of church government reform in 1537, and the city was committed in principle and enforcement to Calvin's moral and social reformist agenda.

Genuine change, though, imposes difficult conditions upon those who must negotiate it. Jesus angered the religious and political leaders of Jerusalem. Amos enraged the satisfied. Martin Luther King Jr. aroused murderous opposition. Calvin spawned less violent but still persistent church, civil, and political enemies in Geneva. When Calvin's supporters fell from power in Geneva, charges of tyranny arose, and Calvin and his reforming ministers were duly warned to keep their noses out of civil and political affairs. As the social climate continued to degenerate into open hostility and opposition, Calvin and Farel were exiled and ordered out of Geneva in 1538. Calvin headed for Strasbourg. His initial attempts at reform in Geneva had failed, but God was not yet finished with the French theologian and social reformer.

Divine Sovereignty and the Light of Divine Care

It is said that humans *pro*pose, but God *dis*poses. The truth of this statement is evident in Calvin's life. Within three years, Calvin was invited back to Geneva, where he resumed and completed his agenda to reform church and society. He had always understood his presence in Geneva as a response to God's call to reconstruct it as a city where God's will was normative in every area of civic life. It was the sovereign will of God that was most important, and that rule of God applied to every arena of human endeavor: economic, educational, industrial, political, ecclesial, and social. Calvin believed that there was no place in all of created order where God's sovereignty did not reach and no place where the bright, clear light of God's divine concern and care could not penetrate. It was the human response to that divine light which concerned Calvin, and his efforts at reform in Geneva were a direct consequence of his doctrine of the Christian life. Calvin saw a moral obligation to structure human life—private, interpersonal, and corporate dimensions—in a way that reflected God's providential care for creation. This spiritual conviction lies at the heart of Calvin's social and political reform.

What is the responsible response to God's love and care? For Calvin, the answer was clear: build a community that honored God by embodying the love, care, and justice of God. Calvin asserted the sociality and interdependence of humanity. By nature, human beings were social and political beings. Therefore, Calvin stressed the communal nature of human experience. The fallen status of humanity due to sin resulted in the broken fellowship of humans with God, and consequently with one another. The corrective, Jesus Christ, was the restorative action of a loving and caring God for humanity. This restoration encompassed the dimensions of both personal (love of God) and social (love of neighbor) renewal. Because of Christ, possibilities now exist for renewed communion with others through new forms of human fellowship and a heightened sense of social responsibility.[9]

Calvin set out with zeal and singleness of purpose to make Geneva the one place where this was evident, to make Geneva a city that honored God. For him, Christian faith and the gospel of Jesus Christ were explicitly relevant to the social realities of the day. In this way, spiritual faith was very pragmatically oriented. As a community responding to God's grace, love, and care, the church's very worship of God served as the grounds for Christian activity in the society. Calvin linked the love of God to love of neighbor, and filtered both through a radical insistence on weaving love and caring into the very fabric of civic life. This called for the legislation of public policy and the creation of public institutions that reflected the divine mandate for unconditional love and caring.

The Witness of Christian Faith in the Care of the World

Like God's pervasive, penetrating light of love and care, reform was for Calvin appropriate in every area of Genevan life—moral, spiritual, and social. There was simply no arena of human social life that Calvin considered out of bounds for reform. Calvin's reform agenda began with the church. For him the church represented the one human community whose very existence embodies God's restorative action in the world. The church's mission was to spread God's penetrating light of love and care into the whole of society, seeking to address spiritual and social problems. In this way the church was indispensable to societal life, concerned not only with matters of personal piety, but also with corporate relations regarding marriage, work, family, and the organization of economic and political life.

Calvin affirmed the necessity for society and its institutions to behave with moral integrity, always exhibiting the care of God for humans who are made in God's image and who are objects of God's love. He affirmed the inseparable connection between spiritual faith and public responsibility. Consequently, he emphatically linked the worship of God to the transformation of public institutions in light of God's sovereign will for human community. Calvin insisted on an educated ministry for the church and an educated citizenry for the society. He called for mandatory, publicly subsidized, liberal, religiously based education for all Genevans. In addition, Calvin founded the Genevan Academy in 1559 to train pastors to the high standards he demanded. He insisted that the academy have not only a faculty of languages and a faculty of theology, but also a faculty of law and a faculty of medicine. He believed that not just preaching but even jurisprudence and surgery were to be undertaken for the glory of God. He influenced minds all over Europe, including the reformer John Knox of Scotland. Calvin's reform efforts in the political arena clearly demonstrated the extent to which his political and legislative agendas were decisively shaped by his theology. Calvin believed that God's sovereignty extended to the whole of creation. Both individuals and the society within which they lived should be designed in accordance with God's will, namely, with love, justice, and care. The sovereignty of God meant that all areas of human living were under the rule and control of God. The state as a political organism was designed to minister to and care for its citizens through its legislation and oversight of civil affairs. The church as a spiritual organism was designed to minister to and care for its citizens by legislating in matters of faith and personal conduct.

Calvin promoted the principle of cooperation between political and spiritual realms, and as a magisterial reformer advocated the use of the resources of the state to aid in reform efforts. Without question, the socially active nature of Calvin's spirituality is evident in his efforts at political and moral reform. He led legislative efforts to produce social regulations to govern personal conduct in the public square. He influenced the city council to pass laws prohibiting immodest apparel and gambling as well as other ordinances regarding education, sanitation, and public discipline. When he turned to the banking and commercial institutions, Calvin was concerned that financial exchange be equitable and fair. In matters of commerce Calvin advocated fair trade legislation to protect citizens, especially the poor, from fraudulent, dishonest, and exploitative commercial exchange. Rome, following Aristotle, had prohibited the charging of interest altogether. Following Matthew 25:27, Calvin persuaded the council to authorize money lending at a moderate rate of interest (except to the poor), a practice that ensured the success of the later Swiss banks, and the growth of that country's economy. He helped to enact policy that protected the poor by remitting interest on money borrowed for necessity items, while charging interest only on money borrowed for luxury purchases. He argued for the need to guarantee work as a God-ordained right for all citizens, and was influential in passing protective child labor laws and fair wages for children. He worked to ensure fair wage and salary compensation in general that would value, respect, and enhance human dignity by enabling workers to meet basic subsistence necessities. He advocated state financial support for orphans, family allowances for ministers, and fair compensation for job-related accidents and injuries. In addition, he believed in the right of all Genevan citizens to enjoy basic health care. In this regard, he worked to develop food laws to guarantee controlled inspection of food quality, preparation, and delivery. He also worked to reform and overhaul Geneva's hospital system to ensure the operation of an effective health care system. That health quality index applied even to the sewer system of Geneva, where Calvin conducted periodic inspections to ensure quality waste management. The laws and procedures that he worked to implement in the area of sewage system reform were hailed as the best throughout Europe and served as a model for other cities.

The concern for the health of Geneva's citizens, as well as that of those traveling through Geneva, in no way reflects an effort to earn salvation. Like Luther and others, Calvin rejected works righteousness.[10] Rather, Calvin's concern with social relevancy and responsibility was a human response to the gracious, restorative action of a loving and caring God who was sovereign over all creation. It was the quest for a responsible response to God's love and care that predisposed him to see the radical implications of spiritual faith for the social and political realms. His faith led to a discovery of God's presence in the sewers as well as the sanctuaries of Geneva. In this way, he highlighted the participatory, engaged nature of spiritual faith as it witnesses to the culture of its day.

6

Call and Response
in Contemporary Life
Martin Luther King Jr.

Divine Call and Vocational Identity

It's alright to talk about "long, white robes over yonder"
. . . but people want some suits and dresses and shoes to
wear down here. It's alright to talk about "streets flowing
with milk and honey," but God has commanded us to be
concerned about the slums down here, and his children
who can't eat three square meals a day.[1]

These are hard words for a rather mild-mannered black Baptist preacher who grew up in the fairly comfortable middle-class section of Atlanta, Georgia, known as the "Sweet Auburn" district in the 1930s and 1940s. This critique of otherworldly, pie-in-the-sky-bye-and-bye religion in favor of a concern for the concrete human condition on earth in the here and now epitomizes Martin Luther King Jr.'s whole approach to religion. What happened in King's life to bring him to this perspective on faith?

King grew up in the heart of southern segregation. As a black man, he witnessed the cruelest expressions of racially based discrimination under the then-current system of racial apartheid known as "Jim Crow." King also experienced, at firsthand, the active resistance to racial oppression mediated through the black religious tradition. As the grandson and son of black preachers, young King was immersed in the rhythms of activist spirituality. He listened to the sermons and hymns of the black church, and imbibed the proactive thrust against segregation—marches, boycotts, organized voter registration efforts—emerging from Ebenezer and other local churches. King saw the liberation ethic intentionally connected to the church's self-understanding. This provided the theological foundation for him to recognize and affirm the potential for revolutionary social change inherent in the Christian gospel.

Early on, King was unsure of his relationship with the church. The idea of becoming a religious professional in the church had little appeal. Although he had been thoroughly immersed in the ministerial ethos, he admitted that, for a long time, he considered law or medicine more suitable vocational possibilities. King, however, could not seem to escape a haunting sense of obligation to become actively involved in the ongoing struggle of blacks to achieve justice in the United States. He wanted to remain connected to the black struggle. He wanted to make a contribution to black freedom. In the midst of this search to find a way to address the tremendous social ills that afflicted blacks, he heard the call of God on his life. Answering this call led him to the ordained ministry. Thus the way he found to engage in the struggle was, ironically, the church.

After completing ministerial training at Crozer Theological Seminary in Chester, Pennsylvania, King entered graduate studies at Boston University as a doctoral student in systematic theology. With course work and comprehensive examinations out of the way, he considered job opportunities. He was offered a teaching position in Detroit. One appeal of this position for King had been that it offered a chance to escape the system of segregation in the South. God had other things in mind. While King was contemplating life in the North, he heard the call of God on his life in the form of a call to a pastoral position at the Dexter Avenue Baptist Church in Montgomery, Alabama. He said yes to God, and returned to the South, not as a "detached spectator" but with a "real desire to do something about the problems" he had personally experienced in his youth.[2]

Barely six months into King's Montgomery job, a black woman named Rosa Parks violated a segregation law by refusing to give up her seat on a bus. The rest was history. King was elected leader and chief spokesperson of a 381-day bus boycott that electrified the American body politic and made him a famous public figure.

King confessed that when he first began in Montgomery, he was searching for God and what God was up to in the world. As he moved through the intense demands of the bus boycott, however, he came to the realization that it was the Spirit of God that had been after him all the time. King would experience the call of God on his life at other times during his brief thirty-nine years, and each time it would come in the midst of unsettling inner doubts about his role in the justice struggle.

In 1963, in the midst of the rubble of the bombed-out Sixteenth Street Baptist Church in Birmingham, Alabama, where four little girls lay dead, King again heard the call of God on his life. This time, he had been privately toying with the idea of stepping down as president of the Southern Christian Leadership Conference and leaving the movement for civil rights to seek a more sedentary and cerebral life as a college professor. But the spirit of the times would not let him do it. He confided to Andrew Young, his chief lieutenant, that "it looks like I'm in this for good."[3]

In 1964, upon receiving the Nobel Peace Prize in Oslo, Norway, King again heard the call of God to expand his horizons on behalf of justice. Observing his son's expanded forays into public confrontations with structural evil, his father, "Daddy" King, concluded that, although he had hoped for Martin's return to quieter, pastoral duties at Ebenezer Baptist Church, where Martin was serving as copastor, "we have lost him to the world."[4] King now saw the world as his parish. The call on his life was relentless and repeatedly led him to a more profound awareness of the strange ways that God continually presses the issue of proactive involvement into the heart of the disciple.

In 1967 King perceived another change in rhythm in his call, leading him beyond the contours of racial matters into the harsh realities of poverty and war. King responded to the succession of calls on his life in the spirit of that great hymn of the church, "Where He Leads Me, I Will Follow." Where King's spiritual consciousness and commitment led him was into the nasty and brutish world of power politics, indiscriminate violence, and socioeconomic disenfranchisement. Awaiting him was the unavoidable mandate to become a cultural worker, a coworker with God, actively engaged in works of love, justice, and peace in the human community.

But King had come to some conclusions about the relationship of God and the gospel to social existence very early on in Montgomery.

Responding to the charge by a segregationist Methodist minister that ministers of the gospel should not be leading bus boycotts because the job of the minister was to "lead souls of men to God, not to bring about confusion by getting tangled up in transitory social problems," King asserted that the gospel of Jesus Christ must be understood as a mandate for active participation in the social issues of the day: "I can see no conflict between our devotion to Jesus Christ and our present action. In fact I see a necessary relationship. If one is truly devoted to the religion of Jesus he will seek to rid the earth of social evils. The gospel is social as well as personal."[5]

Returning to the Birmingham Campaign of 1963 (the zenith year of King's movement), we see his insistence on a socially engaged faith. In the midst of an intense public struggle for social and political justice in Birmingham in 1963, eight clergymen challenged his personal involvement. They argued that the Christian gospel was essentially concerned with the redemption of the soul, and that matters of social concern were outside the boundaries of legitimate faith interests. King's rebuttal relied on what would become the hallmark of his public witness. He said that he was in Birmingham because he had been invited by local organizations to come. He claimed that the invitation was valid because it was in harmony with all such calls to join in the liberation struggles of others. He was in Birmingham in answer to a genuine call to arms as a freedom fighter who understood that the very voice of God was behind the invitation. Like the prophets of old, Jesus, and the apostle Paul, he was answering "a Macedonian call for aid."[6] He understood his own efforts as parallel to the call-response experiences of the Christian narrative. In the final analysis, he argued, he was in Birmingham because injustice was there. It was the most thoroughly segregated city in America. Racial segregation under the system of tripartite social, political, and economic domination of blacks in the South constituted visible corporate evil in its most heinous form. This was injustice institutionalized, and injustice anywhere, said King, represents a threat to justice everywhere.[7] These reasons exhibit King's understanding of Christian faith as a divine manifesto for socially active spirituality.

King was a highly recognizable and public figure. He was a master orator and an innovative Christian theologian. He was widely known for his philosophy of nonviolent direct action, and he has been described as a nonviolent militant, peaceful social activist, apostle of nonviolence, civil rights leader.

Yet King is rarely thought about with reference to his deep commitment to the Christian faith. Hence the "Rev." part is continuously severed from the "Dr." part of him. This is unfortunate because contemporary culture often fails to see the way in which his more visible public actions or "campaigns" for justice (marches, pickets, boycotts, sermons and speeches, jailings, etc.) were undergirded and informed by his theological understanding of and faith commitment to the Christian gospel. Here is a man who went to jail for his beliefs. King's public self-description as "Baptist minister" and private self-description as "democratic socialist" are necessary to understand the underlying motivations that informed King's responses in Birmingham, Montgomery, Selma, and other U.S. cities. King's ethic derived from his self-understanding as a Christian. His proactive engagement with publicly incarnated structures of evil sprang from his faith commitment as a Christian theologian and minister of the gospel. King was a man of deep religious conviction who did what he did primarily out of a spiritual-moral understanding of reality. His faith in the God of Jesus Christ sustained him throughout his twelve years of public witness on behalf of justice.

Call and Response: Asserting the Relevance of Christian Faith

Without question, then, King was an organic spiritualist. That is, he consistently and uncompromisingly accented the prophetic dimension of spirituality, stressing the inseparable connection between the arenas of private faith and public responsibility. In this way he linked the inner, contemplative life of personal, moral redemption to the outer, active life of social, political, and economic transformation. In this way the concern for individual salvation and social liberation were woven together. For King, active participation in the struggle for love, justice, and peace was the only appropriate context for reflection on the meaning of the Christian faith for the culture of modernity.

He believed that there can be no authentic word from or about God that does not emerge from the situation of revolutionary engagement with the forces of sin and evil operating in both individual and corporate structures of society.

King's conception of God was decisive for both his understanding of and response to his vocational call. King repeatedly confessed that his faith in God was the axis around which his life revolved and the source of his continuing hope that the struggle for justice, even if it meant suffering and death, would ultimately succeed. God was going to have the final word in a universe where human sin, despite its virulence and extension, could not prevail. For King, God was essentially radical *agape* in action. As the very essence of God, *agape* was that proactive, life-creating force operating throughout the cosmos and in human history, working to overcome the forces and structures of alienation and oppression. On this view one could say that God's chief revolutionary concern was to restore human community from its fallen, fragmented state. As a cosmic liberator and reconciler, God was radically and inextricably involved in human affairs and intent upon establishing a community of love, justice, and peace. Thus God is radical love, actively involved in human history, using divine power to effect cosmic justice.

King believed that God acted decisively in and through Jesus the Christ. A commitment to the lordship of Jesus was, for King, a commitment to worrying about what God worries about. In Jesus' crucifixion and resurrection, God demonstrated just how radical God was willing to be and act in order to bring human community back to a sense of sanity and wholeness. In Jesus, says King, we find the one who was able to arrive at perfect God-consciousness. This explains the nature, aim, and scope of Jesus' ministry with people on the margins of society, people suffering from political disenfranchisement, psychic dislocation, spiritual confusion, existential emptiness, and physical poverty. In his embrace of *agape* and his focus on God's agenda, Jesus modeled the way the Christian must seek to live under conditions of brokenness and estrangement. Hence, in Jesus, one cannot sever the love of God from the care and concern for one's neighbor. As King saw it, the very confession that "Jesus is Lord" imposed a moral obligation to actively seek out and participate fully in God's work of renewal in both personal and public life. Thus the structure of Jesus' spirituality, attested to in the Gospels, provided the basis for an unequivocal emphasis on the redemption of the social order. For King, Jesus provided the motivating energy for the movement for social justice.

King credits a reading of Walter Rauschenbusch, a Christian pastor working to alleviate horrendous social conditions in Hell's Kitchen in New York in the 1940s and 1950s, for helping him to develop a theological basis for the social concern he had harbored since his youth. King believed that Rauschenbusch had made an invaluable contribution to the Christian church by helping it to see that "the gospel deals with the whole man, not only his soul but his body; not only his spiritual well-bring but his material well-being."[8] Thus, as early as Montgomery, King embraced an understanding of God and the gospel of Jesus that led to his conception of a religion of profound social and political relevance.

> Certainly, otherworldly concerns have a deep and significant place in all religions worthy of the name. . . . But a religion true to its nature must also be concerned about man's social conditions. Religion deals with both earth and heaven, both time and eternity. . . . It seeks not only to integrate men with God but to integrate men with men and each man with himself. This means, at bottom, that the Christian gospel is a two-way road. On the one hand it seeks to change the souls of men, and thereby unite them with God; on the other hand it seeks to change the environmental conditions of men so that the soul will have a chance after it is changed. Any religion that professes to be concerned with the souls of men and is not concerned with the slums that damn them, the economic conditions that strangle them, and the social conditions that cripple them is a dry-as-dust religion. Such a religion is the kind the Marxists like to see—an opiate of the people.[9]

King is clear: religion that focuses solely on the individual to the exclusion of the social lacks the spiritual power to resurrect. It is stagnant, dead, and of little value to God in the work of cosmic redemption. This conviction remained firm throughout his life.

Call and Response: Radical Involvement
and the Quest for the Justice Community

The disciple, made in God's image and committed to God's agenda, is part of a community that affirms the reality of God. This has serious implications for engagement in the social order. *Agape* defines the disciple and the community because God is *agape*. *Agape* structures every human relationship. As King says: "*Agape* is not a weak, passive love. It is love in action. *Agape* is love seeking to preserve and create community. It is insistence on community even when one seeks to break it. *Agape* is a willingness to go to any length to restore community."[10] It was just this kind of love that motivated King in Birmingham in 1963.

When King examined the relationship between God and *agape*, he emerged with a conception of God as radical *agape* in action. In the biblical witness of the exodus and cross events, he saw not only the restoration of broken human community as the ultimate divine concern, but also the lengths to which God is willing to go in order to effect this restoration. God's interest in the affairs of human history is a direct consequence of God's radical love for the world expressing itself through radical, restorative acts of sacrificial self-giving, aimed at the redemption of the social order. This view of God became the hub of King's faith perspective. Thus the actions of the church, those committed to the primacy of the gospel, must be evaluated in light of their consonance with or deviation from the divine agenda.

King's organic spirituality conception of Christian faith and his understanding of God, Jesus, and the gospel provided the foundation for his own intense social and political engagement. He expected the same of any individual Christian or the church as a whole. In fact, for King the authenticity of the Christian life was legitimated through lifestyles that avoided the interiorization as well as the privatization of the faith. Both private and public piety were linked, resulting in the conviction that "other-preservation"—action based upon the notion that one's own destiny remains inseparably connected to the destiny of others—was the first law of life.

For King, life's most persistent question was, "What am I doing for others?"[11] This understanding of the faith generated in him a pronounced intolerance, restlessness, and dissatisfaction with anything that devalued human dignity or denied human freedom. King referred to this as an extremist or maladjusted personality type that refused to conform or accommodate itself to situations of social, political, or economic injustice. The consequences of this personality led inevitably to a rejection of any lifestyle that promoted passivity or indifference in the face of structural evil and massive suffering. For the Christian, such complacency and escapist withdrawal from active public engagement was indicative of a morally irresponsible and spiritually impoverished personality. For King, however, Christian faith represented a grand treatise against the apathetic personality. Apathy, the severing of oneself from engagement with the issues of others, was antithetical to the demands of the gospel. King scoffed at any justification for refusing to confront unjust social and political forces.

The intense anti-apathy emphasis in his faith perspective ultimately led King to embrace, promote, and model a type of radical involvement in society. That is, he emphasized an aggressive participation in the sociopolitics of his day that was driven by a concern to address root causes rather than symptomatic treatments of suffering and injustice. At the same time, he intended to effect a comprehensive transformation of political, social, and economic institutions in light of a particular moral vision fueled and guided primarily by Christian resources. King's radical involvement was predicated on the conviction that God was actively working in history to redeem and restore human community. It was also predicated on the moral obligation to respond properly to the call to join God's reconciling activity in the world. In this way King linked the worship of God and commitment to the gospel of Jesus to active participation in the social order aimed at realizing social, political, and economic justice.[12] Hence King affirmed the inseparable nexus between religion and the human situation, private faith and public responsibility. Guided by a spiritual-moral vision of a beloved community, he became a radical *agape* in action advocate seeking an integrated society where justice is normatively and concretely embodied in the institutional structures of society.

Viewing the church as moral guardian and agent of social transformation, King asserted the church's moral obligation to act as the custodian of revolutionary love and the communal agent of justice. In the final analysis, said King, the decision about participation in human emancipation had already been made at the foot of the cross of Jesus. The church really had no other choice. Thus the Christian community of faith, guided by the norm of *agape*, was for King tantamount to a family of radical *agape* lovers joining God in the work of cosmic redemption. Hence for those involved in the quest for justice, God provided the sustenance for the protracted struggle.

But struggle we must! As steward of the gospel of freedom, the church, in King's view, has inherited the prophetic legacy of activist public critique and social engagement. The church's very existence, then, was a direct result of a collective hearing and answering the call of God to a socially active faith that sought the radical redemption of both the individual and public institutions. Against this ecclesial understanding, King evaluated the authenticity of both individual Christian discipleship and the witness of the church in the context of American racial segregation and violence and the escalating war in Vietnam. When King looked at the role of the church in the struggle against oppression and injustice, he found it severely wanting. The white church and its ministers (along with white liberals), King said, were more adept at the formulation of creedal statements against injustice than becoming actively involved in the struggle. The black church and its ministers, while generally lauded for participation in the struggle for justice, still contained too many apathetic, heaven-oriented ministers, and too many members concerned more with status and class than with justice in the here and now.[13]

King's involvement in this regard grew inevitably from his perceived God-initiated, vocational call on his life. Speaking from the Ebenezer Baptist Church pulpit in 1967, King reminded the congregation that his public activity on behalf of justice could not be severed from his vocational call. "They seem to forget that before I became a civil rights leader, I answered a call which left the Spirit of the Lord upon me and anointed me to preach the gospel."[14]

That sense of vocational call served as the catalyst for King's own vocational response to structural evil in the society. His response focused on the triple evils of racism, poverty, and violence. In the midst of working to recruit volunteers for the antipoverty campaign, King received a request for help in March 1968 from the Reverend James Lawson, a nonviolent tactician who marched and worked with King in several earlier justice campaigns. Lawson and others were involved with an issue of economic justice in Memphis, Tennessee. Fourteen hundred sanitation workers (98 percent of whom were black) had initiated a garbage strike against the city, attempting to create a union to safeguard worker rights and guarantee just incomes. Lawson asked King to come and deliver an inspirational speech to help garner national attention. Against the wishes of his inner circle of advisors, King answered that call and went to Memphis. There, on the balcony of the Lorraine Motel, April 4, 1968, an assassin's bullet ended his life.

Responding to the Call

What good is it, my brothers and sisters, if you say you have faith but do not have works?

James 2:14

God sends the church in the power of the Holy Spirit to share with Christ in establishing God's just, peaceable, and loving rule in the world.

Book of Order, W-7.4001

God's Will for the Church

What do these witnesses of the faith, whose lives we have briefly examined in the preceding chapters, have to tell us about the rhythmic nature of divine call and human response? What do these stories teach us about the nature of engaged piety and the demands of activist spirituality? God seeks the world, not merely the church. "For God so loved the world that he gave his only Son, so that everyone who believes in him may not perish but may have eternal life. Indeed, God did not send the Son into the world to condemn the world, but in order that the world might be saved through him" (John 3:16–17). "All this is from God, who reconciled us to himself through Christ, and has given us the ministry of reconciliation; that is, in Christ God was reconciling the world to himself, not counting their trespasses against them, and entrusting the message of reconciliation to us" (2 Cor. 5:18–19).

According to John, God's love for the world is the basis for God's purposive intervention into human affairs. Cosmic, corporate redemption is God's ultimate goal. This is the final cause for all God's action. Salvation is for the whole world, not just for a privileged few. Paul's second epistle to the community of disciples at Corinth likewise highlights this ultimate objective of God's salvific activity. As God was in Christ, reconciling the world to himself, so the church, the body of Christ, carries the message of reconciliation to the world that God loves and showers with divine interest and concern.

Jesus demonstrated this radical interest and ultimate concern with the world in his brief public ministry. He did not confine himself to any particular group. Rather, he directed his radical message toward the broader society. He expressed an intense concern, almost an anxiety, about the spiritual emptiness, existential brokenness, and psychic dislocation he saw around him. He wept over Jerusalem. He had compassion for the dispossessed and disempowered. He sought out outcasts of all kinds: lepers, the poor, the lame, the diseased. He pronounced bitter public judgments against the elitist, morally self-satisfied authorities.

Jesus' altruistic concern went beyond his own group of followers and even the Jewish community. This concern, for which my mother's invitation to the table is a metaphor (see chapter 1), teaches us that God's invitation is about more than what is immediate, familiar, and safe. God's call is about engagement with the world of the unfamiliar, the alien, the eccentric, the stranger. Faithful response to that call requires a radical involvement in the world, embracing God's agenda, worrying about the things God worries about, loving the people God loves, becoming an agent of God's reconciling love. God's issues include ecological health, economic justice, basic subsistence, adequate education and insurance protection, elimination of divisiveness, freedom from abuse and violence, to name a few. These are the realities about which the church must be concerned simply because this is God's ultimate concern: the restoration of a world that is broken and cannot fix itself due to sin. All good intentions ultimately founder on the reality of human sin. The appeal to goodwill is predicated on high hopes for human perfectability but no appreciation for the power of human sinfulness.

Negating False Dichotomies: The Fallacy
of Dualistic Thinking

Since the church believes that God loves the world and is working toward its redemption, it views the world with a certain optimism. The world is good because it is God's own creation, sustained by God's power, and redeemed by God's love. If the world with all its flaws, inadequacies, and imperfections is good enough for God's love, it is good enough for our love, if we accept God's invitation. The call of God invites us to see the world through God's eyes and become laborers in the vineyard, working toward the consummation of God's agenda: human restoration, societal transformation, and global salvation. The world is the ultimate theater of divine operation. Disciples who respond to God's call must view their lives as instruments in the divine drama of cosmic redemption. This means, again, that the important issues of spiritual formation and faith development must be attentive to both individual and corporate dimensions of the gospel.

In his response to the lawyer's question about which of the commandments is the greatest, Jesus demonstrates remarkable insight into the foundational ethical content of the Jewish legal and prophetic traditions. His provocative summation connects both traditions to *agape* and, in turn, correlates the practice of that love to both the individual and corporate dimensions of the cross. "You shall love the Lord your God with all of your heart, and with all your soul, and with your entire mind. This is the greatest and first commandment. And a second is like it: you shall love your neighbor as yourself. On these two commandments hang all the law and the prophets" (Matt. 22:37b–40).

The gospel of Jesus establishes an inseparable link between spiritual faith and sociopolitical action. Christ exhibited a symbiosis between the interior life of spiritual, God-centered contemplation and the exterior life of bold ethical practice in forgiveness, healing, and seeking justice. In the final analysis, Jesus' reply to the lawyer rejects the seductive and dangerous false dichotomy between an exclusively individual piety and active engagement in the world. With God, the private and public spheres are brought together.

Any ethic based upon the *agape* of the God known in Jesus Christ will be an ethic that promotes a vocation of proactive public engagement.

While church and world remain in dynamic tension, the church's expression of *agape* always takes place in the context of social arrangements of power. Such power is used morally or immorally to develop institutional structures, political agendas, and public policies that impact decisively the lives of people for good or ill. The church's ministry in this world is to bear witness to God's love and vision for the human community.

Although the church may sometimes find itself at odds with the values and practices of the world, it can never dissociate itself from the world. The very nature of the vision and love that the church has to offer cannot be expressed or demonstrated apart from engagement with the world. This is Jesus' primary point. If God is sovereign over all creation, that includes every social, political, and economic realm. The Christian is also a citizen, but a citizen guided by a faith commitment that recognizes the rule of God over all of life. Authentic Christian practice inevitably includes social and political implications that can never be ignored or avoided.

The processes by which humans govern their individual and corporate lives are relevant to the life of the church. The sovereignty of God means that God extends to all of human life. Faith and socio-politics may be different realities, but they can never be divorced because church and world are both under the lordship of God. Because the world enjoys the love of a God who is interested enough to become radically involved in the world's redemption, the church is called to make radical investments in God's agenda of promoting love, justice, and peace in the world.

Christian theology brings to the table of social and political analysis the reality of sin. Christian anthropology views human nature as fallen and all human activity as tragic, open to the possibility of evil. Sin distorts relationships. Christians believe that the primary distortion is in the God-human relationship. Original sin, as Reinhold Niebuhr said, is the denial of our human finitude, the vain attempt by humans to supplant the infinite God. Sin denies the fundamental God-human relationship of Creator and creature. This results in continuous failure to acknowledge God's sovereignty and consent to God's agenda. The warping of values, ideals, ideas, virtues, and visions follows. Since the vertical (divine-human) and horizontal (human-human) relations are inseparably connected, the brokenness and distortion between God and humanity inevitably lead to brokenness and distortion among humans. Christians affirm that this is a lethal dysfunction in all of human life, individual and corporate. Human sinfulness leads to a rejection of God's love and an unwillingness to trust God and to love others. Human motives, including those of Christians, are always mixed, impure, and often blinded by inordinate self-interest. Human relationships, even among Christians, are often characterized by lack of compassion, care, and justice. The result is exploitative relationships, misuse and abuse of power, group hatred, cultural chaos, existential emptiness, poverty, violence, and numerous other forms of distortion.

Paul says: "All this is from God, who reconciled us to himself through Christ, and has given us the ministry of reconciliation; that is, in Christ God was reconciling the world to himself, not counting their trespasses against them, and entrusting the message of reconciliation to us" (2 Cor. 5:18–19). The church, God's agent of reconciliation in the world, is not excluded from a vulnerability to sin. The church includes people subject to the same sinful influences as every other human being. Believers carry the treasure of God's love and vision for humanity in their earthen vessels. When the church falls victim to sin, however, it does not abrogate its call to be God's voice and vision on earth, although it may distort that vision and obscure that call. The church is part of the world, subject to all its vagaries. Its distinction from the world is that it recognizes sin, its own included, and that we all live by grace alone. Furthermore, God has entrusted to the church a message and a mission that no one else has. The church knows it is broken and that the world is broken in a way that the world does not and cannot ever know. God has entrusted God's vision for the world to the church. God empowers the church to act as the agent of God's will on earth. The church should understand that sin lurks even in human efforts for transformation.

James's assertion about the critical linkage between faith and works in the quote that opens this chapter (Jas. 2:14) gets at the heart of the matter. In order to count, faith must respond to the exigencies of the world. Genuine faith is proactively involved in its social and political context. Amos is unequivocal in his condemnation of faith and spirituality disconnected from its social and political context.

Like Jesus after him, Amos criticized the culture of his day, including a moral indictment of the religious community's failure to link its corporate worship of God with its moral responsibility to work toward love, justice, and peace in the public square. Amos is clear: the worship of God is unavoidably linked to joining God in the work of cosmic redemption and building a just, loving, and peaceable human community.[1]

H. Richard Niebuhr has argued persuasively that Christians are to culture as fish are to water.[2] Culture is the medium in which disciples live and express their faith commitments. Culture is the existential reality in which the invitational call of God to radical discipleship is issued, heard, and acted upon. Christians cannot live as detached spectators, beyond the social, political, and economic realities of the world. To attempt this is to become a fish out of water. Church and world, while distinct, remain inseparable arenas of living for Christian citizens.

The "works" of James's "faith without works is also dead" (Jas. 2:26), as interpreted by Amos and Jesus, are actions for love, peace, and justice in the world. Jesus said of himself, quoting Isaiah, "The Spirit of the Lord is upon me, because he has anointed me to bring good news to the poor. He has sent me to proclaim release to the captives and recovery of sight to the blind, to let the oppressed go free, to proclaim the year of the Lord's favor" (Luke 4:18–19). This makes the church's mandate crystal clear. Once this is agreed upon, the only remaining issue is the form that involvement should take in any particular case and the specific ends in view.

Engaged Piety as Nonnegotiable Ethical Demand

The presence of sin in both individual and corporate life requires God's redemptive action in all spheres of human activity. To be sure, God is interested in the salvation of individuals. But individuals participate in structures and institutions that take on a life of their own. As Reinhold Niebuhr has pointed out, men and women may make decisions together that they would not make individually. God seeks to redeem the whole created order, the world and everything in it, individuals and the corporate structures they form. God seeks love and justice not only in individual lives but also in all spheres of social life. Any neat separation of church and world or public and private realms amounts to a false dichotomy. The Christian church claims God's sovereignty over all creation. That sovereignty includes every aspect of the created order, including the world of public life and the numerous institutional arrangements of power, authority, control, and decision making. If the whole world is the sovereign Lord's theater of activity, the ethic of public responsibility is central to the gospel of Jesus Christ. Without question, the invitational call of God to the church inevitably fosters a piety radically engaged in both the public and the private square. An engaged piety emerges as an unavoidable and non-negotiable ethical demand for the church as it responds to God's call to join God in the redemption of the world.

In response to God's call, the church speaks its message of love, hope, and pragmatic witness to a broken world. Like my mother's round of specific daily tasks (see chapter 1) or the rhythmic structure of a jazz composition, the particular form any response may take will vary according to the demands of the context. The call and its telos, however, are everywhere the same: the establishment of the reign of God and its accompanying love and justice in the world.

Viewed in this light, the parable of the Good Samaritan, for example, is not a general teaching about the virtue of individual altruism but an illustration of the reign of God in the world. Jesus shows what God is like and how God acts in the world. At the same time, Jesus shows us how we should be in the world. This parable illustrates in yet another way the inseparable link between our vertical (God) and horizontal (human) relationships. The sum of the law is to love God and neighbor. The lawyer's answer to Jesus' question also sets the priority: first, love God; second, love your neighbor. Love of God is primary; love of neighbor derives from that. This order roots Christian ethics securely in the context of one's relationship with God and not in the context of general altruism. The parable answers the question, Who is my neighbor?

The parable is really about God and the way God's love reaches out to everyone in the world, overcoming all false dichotomies and exclusionary practices. The ethic of care that is lifted up in the narrative is the ethic that expresses God's attitude toward the world and demonstrates how God operates in the world. Christians are morally obligated to embrace this ethic because it is what God is all about. The parable is about how God's love transcends any boundary or dichotomy that divides and fractures the human community. The parable declares that God is active in the life of every person in the world regardless of class, race, culture, gender, politics, or religion.

An authentic Christian response to God's invitational call must be on God's terms, not ours. The pattern is set. There is room for diversity in the particular form of our response but not in the aim of it. God's call to Calvin for love, justice, and care for the world in sixteenth-century Geneva was virtually the same call to Martin Luther King Jr. four hundred years later in Montgomery. Each responded, however, in ways consistent with his own context. As with jazz, there is always room for improvisation and innovation in the response. As we have already said, a vital part of the church's response to God's call is service in the world (*diakonia*). Service in the world in Christ's name is what we mean by engaged piety.

An affirmative response to Christ's invitation has radical implications for how one conducts one's personal and public life. The sacraments of the church enact the gospel in both intensely personal and broader social and political ways. Each sacrament enacts the grace of God and invites our response of gratitude and renewed determination to live our lives in the world before God. The sacraments promote both the private and public nature of discipleship. Baptism marks an individual's inclusion in a community that affirms its mandate to witness to God's reign in the world. The Lord's Supper includes a continual reaffirmation and a rededication to becoming colaborers with God in the work of redeeming and restoring the world, reaffirming the promise made in baptism.

Both sacraments are public enactments of private decisions made in the company of others who know what it means to undertake such risks of faith. Both sacraments involve an individual's communal confession of the lordship of Christ relative to his or her life. Both sacraments are public expressions that signify a continuous yes to God's great invitation to become a willing participant in God's will and way with the world. Both sacraments point inevitably beyond powerful ceremonial experiences to empowering active service in the world. The font and the table serve notice that God remains anxious to reconcile a fragmented world. Public confession of personal and communal shortcomings and personal renewal and corporate recommitment to proactive engagement are core elements of the sacramental experience. Here we are given the opportunity to enter into covenant with God's work in the world particularized in everything from land restoration for the Native American, to economic justice for the poverty-laden, and affordable, quality health care for the uninsured.

Active participation in the sacramental life of the church is propaedeutic to active participation in God's intervention in the world of human affairs. Just as Jesus' own ministry transcended barriers of group, clan, and personal ethics, so the sacraments establish a trajectory that takes the believer into active, risky involvement in the restoration of a broken world. The invitation at the baptismal font and the Lord's Table is for both personal piety and the larger ministry of healing and justice. Such invitations challenge any neat, convenient compartmentalization of life into false dichotomies of secular and sacred. The sacraments challenge the tendency to isolate religious faith from public responsibility. Baptism is not merely an initiation rite but marks the beginning of our Christian ministry as well.

The sacramental invitation makes the world the parish boundary. Limiting church mission to narrowly circumscribed sectarian interests cannot do justice to the comprehensive nature and scope of God's agenda for the world. Both the church budget and the national economy demand the church's scrutiny. Piecemeal philanthropic efforts that are often only remedial attempts to deal with poverty, malnourishment, underemployment, joblessness, crime, and racial intolerance are woefully inadequate in the long term. The challenge and responsibility of an engaged piety is to deal with these issues on as many levels and in as many realms as possible: forming public policy, succoring victims, direct aid, sacrificial giving, to name a few.

In 1997 I served a new church where engaged piety became central to the church's self-understanding. At a congregational meeting dealing with church mission emphases, Lorenzo Burks, a forty-four-year-old father of three, became increasingly frustrated as the discussion progressed. Finally, he could no longer keep silent. He stood up and in an exasperated voice said:

When I joined this church six months ago, I really believed that I was joining something special. I was excited about the possibilities. We all know there is crime, poverty, racism, joblessness, abuse, and gang warfare in this neighborhood. At the very time we could be doing something about all this, you all have spent the last six months mostly trying to get me into the greeting ministry. Well the greeting ministry is okay, and I ain't knockin' it, but that ain't why I joined the church. I want to be part of something relevant in the community. I want to be with a group that offers an alternative lifestyle to what we have now. If it means that I will have to choose between the greeting ministry and community involvement, then let me be clear with y'all right now. To hell with the greeting ministry and to hell with this church!

Though somewhat crudely put, Lorenzo had placed the issue of spiritual relevance squarely before the congregation. The frustration he felt often besets the disciple who discerns the inseparable connection between personal faith and public responsibility. A disengaged piety tends to highlight false dichotomies and to promote either-or instead of both-and choices. The choice between the greeting ministry and community involvement was, of course, a false choice when properly viewed from the standpoint of an engaged piety. As we have seen, this type of piety was at the heart of Calvin's reformist work in Geneva, King's justice efforts in the civil rights movement, Amos's reclamation agenda among the court prophets of Israel, and Jesus' saving witness in ancient Palestine. God's call invites us to reconsider who our neighbor is and then to undertake specific action on behalf of the neighbor in our midst who is without justice and dignity, even when that service may be at some personal cost. God calls us into an active community that is socially and politically involved, working toward the establishment of a just and peaceable social order.

The forms of active engagement may vary, but the mandate is clear. Honesty compels us to admit that this call includes both personal and corporate risk and sacrifice. Sometimes we sign on the dotted line of this covenantal agreement with God and discover that we have no clue about what we are in for.

In 1998 I served as designated pastor of an inner-city church. One Sunday afternoon in a specially called meeting of the Social Action

Committee, one of our church elders, Margaret Steele, discovered the reality of risk and cost. The committee wanted to address the homelessness and hunger issues in the community, but could never get beyond written resolutions, newspaper articles, and verbal pronouncements. Toward the end of the meeting, Margaret announced that she had been thinking and praying about the issue for a long while, and decided she was going to give up talking about it and just do some "real ministry." She said she was tired of drafting papers and positions and then going home to eat her well-prepared meal in her nice home while people were starving in the community. The other committee members and I (as pastor) were stunned. She then invited any of us who wished to join her to follow her to Sears, where she purchased two huge stainless steel pots, four large spoons, and a supply of plastic bowls and spoons. Then she drove to the local Kroger store and bought all the chili fixings available. She then drove to the Food Rite and bought more chili fixings. She called her husband and told him to get the stove and the family van ready. She cooked chili, loaded it in her van, and, along with her husband, two boys, and three of us from the committee, drove downtown and served hungry and homeless persons chili out of her van. The police came by, asked her to stop, and when she refused, ticketed and then arrested her. As they took her away, she shouted to us from the back seat of the police car to keep on serving until all the chili was gone.

Margaret and her husband Harold paid fines, returned with their chili van, paid more fines, until eventually they obtained a license to distribute food from a mobile vehicle. Why did they do this? They both said they did this out of their own spiritual commitment to the gospel of Jesus Christ and his love for others. Margaret and Harold were willing to pay the heavy cost that an engaged piety sometimes exacts. Other members of the Social Action Committee were challenged to become involved in other ways. The mandate to be radically involved in the lives of the neighbor had become inescapable.

Theologians Johannes Metz and Jürgen Moltmann point out that an engaged piety never allows us to forget that Jesus Christ was crucified not between two candlesticks on a church altar but between two criminals on a garbage dump outside the city limits of Jerusalem.[3] Dietrich Bonhoeffer states it succinctly, "when Christ calls a man or a woman, Christ bids that person come and die."[4] The invitational call of God, like Mama Dorothy's dinner call to the Ivory household, is ultimately a call for active engagement in the world. It is a call that seeks relevance through the demands of radical involvement with the context. The gospel of Jesus Christ demands an engaged piety, a socially active faith that is concerned with the ultimate redemption of the social order in accordance with God's vision of justice and peace. The mystery of faith is this: Christ has died; Christ is risen; Christ will come again. Let us show our gratitude for God's redeeming grace by being active in the world God created, loves, and seeks, for the sake of healing and justice.

Notes

Chapter 1

1. *The Constitution of the Presbyterian Church (U.S.A.)*, Part II, *Book of Order* (Louisville, KY: Office of the General Assembly, 1999), G-1.0200.
2. John Calvin, *Institutes of the Christian Religion*, 1.14.1; ed. John T. McNeill, trans. Ford Lewis Battles, 2 vols., Library of Christian Classics (Philadelphia: Westminster, 1960), 1:160.
3. Ibid.

Chapter 2

1. Dieter Hessel, *Social Ministry* (Philadelphia: Westminster, 1982), 27–30. See also Dieter Hessel, and Larry Rasmussen, eds., *Earth Habitat: Eco-Justice and the Church's Response* (Minneapolis: Fortress, 2001); C. Eric Lincoln and Lawrence H. Mamiya, *The Black Church in the African-American Experience* (Durham, NC: Duke University Press, 1990); Niles Preman, *Resisting the Threats to Life: Covenanting for Justice, Peace, and the Integrity of Creation* (Geneva: WCC Publications, 1989); Brian E. Fogarty, *War, Peace, and the Social Order* (Boulder, CO: Westview Press, 2000).
2. See John Calvin's discussion of *pietas* in the Christian life in *Institutes of the Christian Religion*, 1.2.
3. See Claude Welch, *Protestant Thought in the Nineteenth Century*, vol. 1: 1799–1870 (New Haven, CT: Yale University Press, 1972), 22–30.
4. *The Constitution of the Presbyterian Church (U.S.A.)*, Part II, *Book of Order* (Louisville, KY: Office of the General Assembly, 1999), G-1.0200.
5. Ibid., G-2.0500, G-3.000.
6. See *The Constitution of the Presbyterian Church (U.S.A.)*, Part I, *Book of Confessions, The Confession of 1967* (Louisville, KY: Office of the General Assembly, 1999).
7. See *Facing Racism: Search for the Beloved Community*, policy document of the Presbyterian Church (U.S.A.) (Louisville, KY: Office of the General Assembly, 1999).

Chapter 4

1. See Richard A. Norris, ed., *The Christological Controversy*, Sources of Early Christian Thought (Philadelphia: Fortress Press, 1980); Gerald O'Collins, *Christology: A Biblical, Historical, and Systematic Study of Christ* (New York: Oxford University Press, 1995); Jaroslav Pelikan, *Jesus Through the Centuries* (New Haven, CT: Yale University Press, 1985).

2. See *The Constitution of the Presbyterian Church (U.S.A.)*, Part II, *Book of Order* (Louisville, KY: Office of the General Assembly, 1999), G-1.0100. This is an expression of the universal Christian community's understanding of the lordship of Jesus Christ and his role as head of the church, a view of Jesus Christ universally held among Christian believers regardless of particular denominational focus.

3. For an insightful analysis of the Jesus Seminar and its implications for believing in Jesus Christ, see Leanne Van Dyke, *Believing in Jesus Christ* (Louisville, KY: Geneva Press, 2002).

4. Marcus Borg, *Meeting Jesus Again for the First Time* (San Francisco: Harper, 1994), 30.

5. On sacramental theology in the Christian tradition see Geoffrey Wainwright, "Eucharist and/as Ethics," *Worship* 68 (1994): 194–210; William Cavanaugh, *Torture and Eucharist: Theology, Politics and the Body of Christ*, Challenge in Contemporary Theology (New York: Blackwell, 1998); Arthur A. Just, *The Ongoing Feast: Table Fellowship and Eschatology at Emmaus* (Collegeville, MN: Liturgical Press, 1993); Jean-Marie Tillard, *Flesh of the Church, Flesh of Christ: At the Source of the Ecclesiology of Communion* (Collegeville, MN: Liturgical Press, 2001).

Chapter 5

1. Calvin on Hos. 6:6, in *Calvin: Commentaries*, trans. and ed. Joseph Haroutunian, Library of Christian Classics 23 (Philadelphia: Westminster Press, 1958), 139.

2. Ibid., 360, Calvin on the implications of Gen. 18:19 for Christian ethics in the common life.

3. *A Life of John Calvin* (Oxford: Blackwell, 1990), xi.

4. Ibid., p. xi–xii.

5. See Martin Luther King Jr., *Strength to Love* (Philadelphia: Fortress, 1963), 17–25, 96–105, 127–37, 138–46; Allan Boesak, *Black and Reformed: Apartheid, Liberation, and the Calvinist Tradition* (Maryknoll, NY: Orbis, 1984).

6. John Calvin, *Commentary on the Book of Psalms* (Edinburgh: The Calvin Translation Society, 1845), xlii–xliv.

7. See William Stevenson, *The Story of the Reformation* (Richmond, VA: John Knox Press, 1959), 66–71; and *Calvin: Commentaries*, trans. and ed. Joseph Haroutunian, Library of Christian Classics 23 (Philadelphia: Westminster, 1958), 51–58.
8. See Stevenson, *Story of the Reformation*, 16–65.
9. For a fascinating discussion of Calvin's sense of societal responsibility, see André Bieler, *Calvin's Economic and Social Thought*, ed. Edward Dommen, trans. James Greig (Geneva: World Alliance of Reformed Churches, 2005).
10. See *Calvin: Commentaries*, 314ff. Here Calvin offers a more lengthy treatment of ethics and the common life for the Christian, including works righteousness.

Chapter 6

1. "I See the Promised Land," in *A Testament of Hope: The Essential Writings of Martin Luther King, Jr.*, ed. James Melvin Washington (San Francisco: Harper and Row, 1986), 282.
2. Martin Luther King Jr., *Stride toward Freedom: The Montgomery Story* (San Francisco: Harper and Row, 1958), chapter 1.
3. See Taylor Branch, *Parting the Waters: America in the King Years 1954–63* (New York: Simon & Schuster, 1989), 889–94, 900–902.
4. "Eyes on the Prize—America's Civil Rights Years," "1963," and "Ain't Scared of Your Jails," ed. Henry Hampton, Audiovisual Library.
5. King, *Stride toward Freedom,* 116–17.
6. See "Letter from Birmingham City Jail," in *Testament of Hope*, 290.
7. Ibid.
8. King, *Stride toward Freedom*, 91.
9. Ibid., 36.
10. *Testament of Hope*, 20.
11. Luther D. Ivory, *Toward a Theology of Radical Involvement: The Theological Legacy of Martin Luther King Jr.* (Nashville: Abingdon, 1997), 67.
12. Ibid., 110, 123–24.
13. See King, *Stride toward Freedom;* 425–29, 447–50; "Letter from Birmingham City Jail," 245–301; and "Knock at Midnight," 498–502, in *Testament of Hope*.
14. See "Promised Land," in the audiovisual series *Eyes on the Prize*.

Chapter 7

1. See chapter 3 above on Amos.
2. See H. Richard Niebuhr, *Christ and Culture* (New York: Harper & Brothers, 1951), 10–11, 32, 39, 69–72.

3.   See Jürgen Moltmann, *The Crucified God*, trans. R. A. Wilson and John Bowden (New York: Harper & Row, 1974), 5, 131–32, 204, 246, 256, 322.

4.   Bonhoeffer, *Discipleship*, ed. Geoffrey B. Kelly and John D. Godsey, trans. Barbara Green and Reinhard Krauss, Dietrich Bonhoeffer Works 4 (Minneapolis: Fortress, 2001), 44–45, 51, 87.